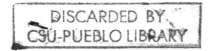

To Lucy,

with love & best wishes,

A souvenir of your visit,

19th July 1990.

Olga

# GRETNA GREEN

*A Romantic History*

## Also by Olga Sinclair

*Man at the Manor*
*Man of the River*
*Hearts by the Tower*
*Bitter Sweet Summer*
*Wild Dreams*
*My Dear Fugitive*
*Never Fall in Love*
*Master of Melthorpe*
*Tenant of Binningham Hall*
*Where the Cigale Sings*
*Gypsy Julie*
*Orchids from the Orient*
*When Wherries Sailed By*
*Gypsies*
*Dancing in Britain*
*Children's Games*
*Toys and Toymakers*
*Gypsy Girl*

### as Olga Daniels
*Lord of Leet Castle*
*The Gretna Bride*
*The Bride From Faraway*
*The Untamed Bride*

### as Ellen Clare
*Ripening Vine*

# GRETNA GREEN

## A Romantic History

OLGA SINCLAIR

UNWIN HYMAN

HYMAN

LONDON SYDNEY WELLINGTON

First published in Great Britain by the Trade Division of Unwin Hyman
Limited, in 1989.

**UNWIN HYMAN LIMITED**
15–17 Broadwick Street, London W1V 1FP

Allen & Unwin Australia Pty Ltd
8 Napier Street, North Sydney, NSW 2060, Australia

Allen & Unwin New Zealand Pty Ltd with the Port Nicholson Press
60 Cambridge Terrace, Wellington, New Zealand

---

**British Library Cataloguing in Publication Data**

Sinclair, Olga
    Gretna Green.
1. Scotland. Dumfries and Galloway Region.
Gretna Green. Clandestine marriage, 1770–
I. Title
306.8′1′0941483
ISBN 0-04-440328-3

---

Typeset in 11 on 12 point Ehrhardt by Cambridge Photosetting Services
and printed in Great Britain at The University Press, Cambridge

# Contents

*The Author and Publishers would like to thank:*

The Duke of St Albans; The Earl of Jersey; Sir Charles Nightingale; Sir James Goldsmith; Mr R Adair Houston; Miss Pat Bryden; Mrs Shirley Moore; Mrs Dorothy Taylor; Mr Jim Jackson; The late Mr Andie Duncanson; Mr & Mrs Charles Morton; Mrs Jean Sturrock; Mrs Hilda (Shroder) Armitage; Mr & Mrs Norman Lord; Mr & Mrs David Cooper; Mr & Mrs Ray Searle; Mr & Mrs Michael Ware; Mr & Mrs A K Brunt; The Rev J Pagan; Mr Adam Barr; Mr & Mrs M Phillips; Mrs Celia Conway; Mr & Mrs D Kenyon; Gretna Constabulary; The Scottish Record Office. The librarians of many counties particularly: The Ewart Library, Dumfries; Norwich Central Library; also those of Annan, Devon, Hounslow, Gloucester, Carlisle, Durham, Cambridgeshire, Lincolnshire, Newcastle and the Mitchell Library, Glasgow. And many other people who gave help so generously in so many different ways.

Also, Steven Matthews and Dumfriesshire Newspapers and Don Donabie, Gretna, for the use of certain photographs.

# List of Illustrations

between pages 50 and 51

The Old Blacksmith's Shop
A mock wedding
Sarah Anne Child by Romney
John Fane, Earl of Westmorland by Romney
A Fleet Wedding
Miss Pat Bryden
Gretna Hall
Joseph Pasley
David Lang
'Fillial Affection' by Rowlandson
Henry Brougham by Lawrence
John Peel
Neville King and Joan Lambert
The Sark Tollbar
Kitty Barnes by Holmes
Thomas, Lord Cochrane by Stroehling

between pages 114 and 115

'The Red-Hot Marriage'
Eileen Gailey and Bishla Gorzynski
Keith and Amanda Brunt
Edward Gibbon Wakefield
'One Mile from Gretna'
Thomas Johnston
'Granny' Graham
Mr Mackintosh
The Dutch Giant
Last minute bid to stop a wedding
'To the Lord or Count of Gretna Green'
Agnes and Norman Lord
James and Isabel Goldsmith
Sir James Goldsmith and his daughter Isabel

xi

*Gretna Green*

Jan and Dave Cooper
Robert and Brenda Simpson
Jeff Brown and Diane Ridley
'The Reconciliation'

**To Stan**
who has supported and
encouraged me always.

Oh, gallop along with a right merry song,
   Through wood and vale and hollow,
The turnpike men may shake their heads,
   And half the world may follow;
But I care not what the old folks say,
   I'll take no heed or warning,
For I'll be wearing a wedding-ring,
   At Gretna in the morning.

*Popular song*

CHAPTER ONE

# The Tourist's Gretna Green

Mention Gretna Green and almost inevitably it raises a smile, a chuckle, not quite a dirty laugh, but certainly a mischievous grin. Everybody has heard of the place, if only from a snippet of romantic sensationalism in one of the Sunday papers. The historical facts that thrust fame – some would say notoriety – upon it as the 'village of runaway marriages' are less well-known.

When it comes to marriage the Scots are far from dour. On that question they have never needed devolution to keep themselves apart from the much more canny English, Welsh and Irish, not to mention the rest of the continent of Europe. Sixteen, they decided, was old enough for a laddie and his lass to know if they were truly in love and so it remains to this day. 'Twenty-one,' said the Sassenachs, and stuck to their guns over the point for more than 200 years, but it was they who gave in, partially, in the end. Today, young adults over the age of eighteen find it unthinkable that they should not be allowed to marry whom they choose. Yet this was the position from 1754 until 1970; it led to some of the most romantic, bizarre, infamous and exciting escapades ever recorded, being acted out in the quiet little village of Gretna Green.

In those days it was just not done for a couple to live together unless they were married, and parents had the power to forbid a marriage which only the magistrates' courts could overrule. So, for many couples, there seemed to be only one way out and that was to run away to a country with more liberal laws – and that meant to Scotland. In fact, they could have been married anywhere in that country, but the place with the reputation for marriages was Gretna Green.

Gretna Green lies just over the border of Scotland, the first place on the road from London and the south of England, and this simple geographical fact allowed the village to take full advantage of the variations between the marriage laws of the two countries. It became a

1

'safety-valve' for hundreds of couples, determined to marry to please themselves and ensured that the name of the village should be known all over the world.

Other countries had their own special places which achieved some renown for providing facilities for quick and easy marriages, notably Elkton in Maryland, USA. Elkton lies just south of the state border with Pennsylvania and within easy reach of New York, and it was the laws of neighbouring states that brought lovers pouring into Elkton. In both Scotland and Maryland, there were people only too eager and often not too scrupulous about cashing in on the 'trade', and many bizarre characters sprang into prominence. Soon Elkton became known as the Gretna Green of America but its story goes back only to 1913, while the Scottish village has its roots way back in the history of early civilisation.

A ceremony of marriage within the Church was instituted during the very beginnings of Christianity and was generally used throughout the various parts of Britain but it had no greater validity in the eyes of the law than the old form of irregular marriage. This was so-called because it was not conducted according to the accepted form of either the civil or the religious authorities. It was a contract, verbal or written, between two consenting 'adults' which, properly witnessed, was absolutely binding and acceptable in law. Irregular marriages were outlawed in England by Lord Hardwicke's Marriage Act of 1754 but remained legal in Scotland until 1940. Generally speaking thereafter, marriages were required to be conducted in church or in a Register Office but one important difference remained unique to Scotland. There, anyone over the age of sixteen could marry without parental consent while in virtually the whole of the rest of Europe, twenty-one was the age of maturity and in some countries it was even older.

The couples who gave the aura of romance to Gretna were not those who lived there but those who came fleetingly by chaise, on foot or on horseback. More recently, they have travelled by train, car, motorbike, plane or even helicopter. They made their vows and returned to whence they came, to every corner of the British Isles and to every country of Europe or further afield, throughout the world. Who were – and are – these breakers of convention? What happened to those who briefly stole the headlines and whose stories have remained in the rag-bag of public memory?

While some of the inhabitants of Gretna held up their hands in horror at such 'goings on', others felt a warm sympathy for the couples who continually arrived, so much in love and so determined to become man and wife in the face of all opposition. Not surprisingly, there were always a number of entrepreneurs ready and willing to make money by meeting their demands. Events of the past two hundred and fifty years reveal how

Jim Jackson, the guide at the Gretna Hall Blacksmith's Shop gives his whole heart to his job. He never uses the words 'mock' marriages – to him they are anvil weddings and are either for fun or for love. He has a wry sense of humour as he reflects on the variety of people who come, individually or in busloads, every day throughout the season. 'Some spend an hour here and say it's been the most interesting part of their holiday – others look in and when they see it costs thirty pence they turn and run. You'd think I was going to attack them!'

history repeats itself while outwardly seeming to change. Every generation has produced its rebels, and there have always been those who applauded and those who were shocked. Financial gain has played an important part, too, in the roles of the lovers and the people who helped them, as well as with pursuing parents. That truth is stranger than fiction is borne out by the happenings in and around Gretna.

The village lies in the county of Dumfriesshire, immediately north of the border with England. The old road, now bypassed, runs through a street of plain clean-scrubbed houses, which have the appearance of very respectable matrons who cannot quite live down their colourful past. Many are actually in the village of Springfield and date from the last century. A newer part of Gretna sprang up around a cordite factory built there during the First World War, it was chosen because the site was remote and unlovely – expendable almost. Gretna Green itself is merely a small collection of cottages around the crossroads. There is a one-time blacksmith's, a church, an hotel and a disused railway station, all of which played their part in the elopements. Now, every year about half a million people stop off to gaze at these scenes which symbolise so much of the old irregular marriages, and the place vies with Loch Ness as a major tourist attraction.

Prominent at the crossroads stands the white-washed cottage and former smithy where a painted sign declares 'This is the World Famous Old Blacksmith's Shop, Marriage Room'. It was from this point, at the Headlesscross, that the old coaching road ran southwards to Carlisle, and the low cottage dates from the early eighteenth century. The Smithy, reached through a turnstile, displays a collection of relics from the 'marriage-trade', with the anvil prominently featured. There are bellows, farm implements and plenty of horse-shoes, paintings, prints and photographs of former 'priests', and cartoons and lithographs of irregular wedding ceremonies. The real proof of the Smithy's past lies in the old marriage registers, carefully filled in by the acting 'priest'. A mass of newspaper cuttings, yellowed with age, report stories of elopements and anniversaries and the visits of kings and queens and other famous people. Less well-known visitors have made their mark by writing names, initials and dates on the walls in places that make one marvel at their agility and ingenuity. The collection of horse-drawn vehicles may also be justified as belonging to the history of Gretna, for undoubtedly, over the years, every possible conveyance was used to transport the bridal parties.

At the back of the Gretna Hall Hotel is a second blacksmith's shop, but this one was converted from a coach-house in 1938 as part of the blacksmith myth. Weddings were held there for two years before the law was changed, and now it also operates as a museum.

The term 'blacksmith's marriage' seems to have been a synonym for irregular marriage for at least 300 years. In England, as well as in Scotland, this symbol appears to have been adopted as a result of popular belief rather than by any historical fact. There are records of 'priests' at Gretna who came to their calling from a variety of different trades – soldier, fisherman, smuggler, stonemason, cobbler, weaver, farm-labourer, valet, pedlar and piper – but not one of them was really the brawny man in leather apron, alternately fashioning ironwork and wedding bonds over his anvil. Nor, indeed, was any one of them an ordained priest. Yet so common was this misnomer that lawyers conducting cases in which evidence of a Scottish irregular marriage was a crucial fact, took sarcastic delight in referring to their witness as 'Mr Blacksmith'.

The Smithy was certainly an established business from at least the beginning of the eighteenth century. The glow of the blacksmith's fires and the ring of his hammer on the anvil were familiar sights and sounds in his workshop adjoining the little whitewalled cottage at the Headless-cross. But at that time, marriages usually took place in the village inns, in private houses or even out of doors among the gorse bushes. Later on, thousands of people were married in the blacksmith's shops, but not, so far as is recorded, by a real blacksmith.

The Gretna Hall Hotel which proclaims itself as the 'Original Marriage House' has an authentic and notable association with runaway marriages, dating from the time when it was converted from a private house into a coaching inn at the end of the eighteenth century. Among those who were married in what is now the reception hall are the names of some of the oldest and most aristocratic families, not only in Britain but in Europe as well. Another museum dedicated to the old 'marriage-trade' is the Sark Bridge Tollbar where large letters bear the legend

Duane & Nicky Snelling of Eastleigh, Hants were married on 13 June 1988. They were not runaways, they had told their parents they were going to Gretna to be married. They just wanted to have a quiet wedding on their own. But when, after the Register Office ceremony, they walked into the Blacksmith's Shop, they were watched by a party of twenty-four tourists from Holland.

Jim invited the couple to stand, holding hands over the anvil and spoke with solemnity and sincerity. 'You are here in the Blacksmith's Shop to reaffirm your marriage vows and in doing so you become, yourselves, part of the history and tradition of Gretna Green, and your witnesses are not only we, who are here with you, your witnesses are also the countless thousands who over the centuries have made the same journey with the same aim. As the blacksmith joined two metals together over the anvil and made them one, so I now join two lives together, never to be parted.' He clanged the hammer resoundingly on the anvil and just before the photographers moved in, the whole Dutch party spontaneously burst into a song of congratulations in their own language.

'Over 10,000 marriages took place here'. When the first bridge was built over the Sark Water in 1818, this museum, a cottage known originally as Allison's Bank Toll, was the first house on the Scottish side of the border. Because marrying was such a lucrative business, this excellent location was soon seized upon for its convenience in capturing the custom of any likely runaways. Competition among rival 'priests' was keen and so its proximity to the border an obvious tactical advantage, at a time when most clients came by road from the south. Later there was a railway, but that is another chapter in the ever changing scene of Gretna.

For the majority of tourists the visit to Gretna is no more than a light-hearted hour. The music of the pipes swirls over the car-park as they drive up and pose for snapshots beside the kilted, puff-cheeked piper, and the guides to the museums have a fund of stories, fantastic, incredible, scandalous, bizarre and romantic. As part of the fun two members of each party are pulled forward to participate in a mock marriage. A good guide enhances the humour by selecting his bride and groom judiciously, pairing the most ill-matched or the most extrovert, dressing the bride up in a veil and handing her a bouquet of plastic flowers – 'Fresh cut this morning!' The groom has a grey topper and that of his best man falls right over his eyes and ears. Some of the story of Gretna Green is told and an interpreter explains the jokes to continental parties. They are told of the introduction of Lord Brougham's Marriage Act which introduced a three week wait, a 'cooling off period', which gets a laugh in any language. They ask the couple, often pensioners, if they are over sixteen, hands are joined and a brass ring is produced which is about two inches in diameter. 'Will you take this woman to be your awful wedded wife?' Clang! The hammer rings sharply on the anvil. 'Now the moment you've all been waiting for – you may kiss the bride.' It all takes about fifteen minutes and with a good party, the laughter peals out spontaneously and constantly as everyone is in a holiday mood.

The farce is a good excuse to take photographs of all the company, carefully arranged around those playing the parts; the father of the bride is given a shot-gun because 'that's the sort of wedding it is!' During the height of the season the parody is re-enacted fifteen or twenty times a day in each of the smithies, with guides taking the role of the 'priest'. Admittedly those on package tours are a captive audience, whether they are British, American, Japanese, Israeli or from other foreign parts, their itinerary was mapped out before they first glanced at the brochure. Tour operators know that the visit to Gretna holds a strange fascination and provides their clients with amusement and interest as well as the chance to buy another souvenir.

Every now and again however a couple turns up who really were married there, and the raillery is suddenly hushed. An undercurrent of excitement quivers through the crowded room as that which was ridiculous and hilarious is discovered to have a core of truth and reality. Curiosity, a touch of sentimentality, of tenderness and wonder, changes the mood. Cameras flash to capture the smile of the elderly lady who stands, plumply blushing beside her grey-haired husband, holding hands again, and recalling that around fifty years ago they were married by Mr Richard Rennison, the last in a long line of irregular 'priests', on that very spot. After a lifetime together they have come back and the publicity, the attention and interest catch them unawares.

'I felt like a VIP,' said one lady. 'We had to kiss over the anvil while people took pictures and I was asked to sign autographs.'

How do they fit into the picture of rebellious teenagers? Why did they defy convention, risk everything for love and do it their way? Over and over again the Gretna story is repeated, yet every time it is different and there are as many variations of the theme as there are lovers. Were all the girls pregnant? Were they too young to know their own minds? Were they just self-centred, defying their parents' wishes, and did they regret their rashness – marry in haste and repent at leisure? In fact, was it in haste at all?

Linda Eastwood from Canada and Ron Whitling from Australia, who were on holiday in Britain, chanced to book the same coach tour of Scotland. They hardly noticed each other as they travelled through its spectacular mountains and glens – until, almost at the end of their trip, they made the routine stop at the Old Blacksmith's Shop, and were picked at random to be bride and groom at a mock anvil wedding.

'I think they asked us to do it because we were the only single people on the tour,' said Linda. 'I was a bit embarrassed at first, but once it got started it was great fun.'

That 'marriage' was the catalyst. Next day, as the coach sped south towards London, Ron moved over to sit beside Linda and they chatted all the way. When they arrived he asked, 'Can I see you some more?' Linda agreed and between rushed visits to their various relatives, they got to know each other better.

Just before Linda flew home to Canada Ron proposed, and she accepted. 'I was looking for a happy holiday, but I never expected to fall in love,' said Linda.

Some of the elopements are so well documented that it is possible to reconstruct them with great accuracy, even including actual dialogue, stilted and unreal as some of those old-fashioned phrases sound to our ears today. Of others only the barest facts are recorded, a few have been stiffled even from the pages of *Debrett* and some did not come to light until many years after they happened.

The history of Gretna is not straightforward, it is not just a steady stream of marriages but the story of several sensational elopements, often of rich or aristocratic or famous people. The gossip columnists of the eighteenth or nineteenth centuries were every bit as alert to stories of passion and scandal as they are in the twentieth, always seeking to titillate their readers. 'All the world loves a lover' and even more so if that lover is causing embarrassment to a well-known, rich and pompous parent! To the young such escapades have shown the way, opened up possibilities and led a trend that has had a snowball effect so that, from time to time, Gretna has found itself swamped with runaway couples. This has been followed by pleas and demands for legislation to halt the flow and leave the border village to its own peaceful affairs. As a result, laws have been changed, but they have never quite been brought into line with those of England, and though those laws have always been universal throughout Scotland, Gretna has invariably dominated the 'marriage-trade'.

A letter addressed to 'The place where they marry, Scotland' will unhesitatingly be delivered to the Register Office in Gretna. Every year the number of marriages there is considerably larger than those of births or deaths. A marriage in Scotland is recognised as legally binding in every country in Europe with the exception of Russia, and its validity has been fiercely defended by Scottish lawyers over the centuries.

With the passing of every new law it has been confidently predicted that the role of Gretna Green as *the* marriage centre is over but to date that has not happened. In fact, new legislation on marriages in Scotland came into force on 1 January 1978 and almost immediately the number of weddings at the Register Office began to rise again.

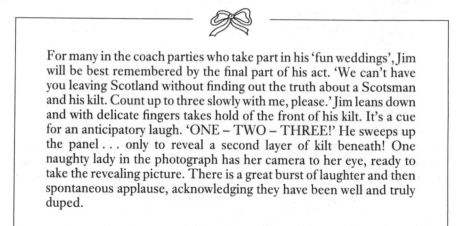

For many in the coach parties who take part in his 'fun weddings', Jim will be best remembered by the final part of his act. 'We can't have you leaving Scotland without finding out the truth about a Scotsman and his kilt. Count up to three slowly with me, please.' Jim leans down and with delicate fingers takes hold of the front of his kilt. It's a cue for an anticipatory laugh. 'ONE – TWO – THREE!' He sweeps up the panel . . . only to reveal a second layer of kilt beneath! One naughty lady in the photograph has her camera to her eye, ready to take the revealing picture. There is a great burst of laughter and then spontaneous applause, acknowledging they have been well and truly duped.

CHAPTER TWO

# Sarah Anne Child and the Earl of Westmorland

Of the early elopements to Gretna Green the most sensational and romantic was that of Sarah Anne Child and John Fane, 10th Earl of Westmorland, in 1782. They set a style that was difficult to improve upon, though many girls were inspired by Sarah Anne's example, including her own granddaughter.

Sarah Anne was the daughter and sole heiress of Robert Child, an enormously wealthy London banker and the principal director of Child's Bank. She grew up in the luxury of the family home at 38 Berkeley Square in London, and surrounded by the opulence of their country estate, Osterley Park in Middlesex. The old Tudor house at Osterley had been bought by her great-grandfather with the intention of using the vaults under the courtyard for storing the bank's cash. The magnificent cedar trees that now stand between the lake and the house are believed to have been planted to celebrate the birth of Sarah Anne in 1764.

Sarah Anne was about seventeen or eighteen when she first met the handsome young Guards officer, for whom she was prepared to relinquish all. Lord Westmorland was then twenty-three, he had succeeded to the earldom at the age of fifteen, and his family seat was Apethorpe Hall in Northamptonshire, a house which was modest in comparison to Osterley. It has been suggested that his acquaintance with Robert Child began when, as a rather impecunious young officer, he sought a loan from the great banker. Business was conducted in a gentlemanly way and on occasions Mr Child invited the young Earl to dine with him, but he had no illusions as to his means. There are no records of meetings between Sarah Anne and the Earl, but doubtless they attended many of the same routs, balls and other social functions, and without a doubt a loving relationship developed between them. But there seemed to be no hope of Robert Child agreeing to such a match since he was determined that his daughter should marry a man suitable to

9

Among the eminent names listed in the Queen's birthday honours in June 1988, was that of Miss Pat Bryden, Registrar of Gretna, who was made a Member of the British Empire. There could hardly have been a more popular announcement just over the border. 'The matchmaker. MBE for Pat – Gretna's world famous Registrar', the Annandale Observer announced with pride.

Pat Bryden was born and bred in Gretna, and has been officiating at weddings there since 1955. Remembering the first marriage she ever did she said, 'I was probably more nervous than the couple. I thought, I'll never do it. My boss said choose the couple for yourself. I picked a couple from Oswaldtwistle and they were small and nervous, and I thought if they're not very sure, and I'm not very sure, between us we'll manage to make something of it.'

Since then she has married well over 9,000 couples, yet time and time again it is said of her: 'She makes weddings feel so special.' She became registrar in 1975 – her previous applications for the post having been turned down because the job was traditionally held by a male.

Now there are people in every corner of Britain, and in far away places all over the world, who know her and remember her. She has sometimes been called upon to give live radio interviews by telephone, taking part in programmes in Australia, Canada and America. Most of the people she has married have come from outside the village, but so many of those weddings have had that touch of the unusual that almost every week her face is seen smiling from the local paper, her hands lightly resting on the shoulders of some happy couple, whose marriage has made a story.

carry on the banking business, and those plans did not include a fortune-hunting aristocrat.

Despite her father's disapproval, Sarah Anne contrived to meet her dashing young suitor and when there seemed to be no other hope, they planned their elopement. A few days before, one afternoon in May 1782, Lord Westmorland dined with Robert Child at Temple Bar. Audaciously he turned the conversation towards marriage.

'Child,' he said, 'suppose you were in love with a girl and her father refused his consent to the union, what should *you* do?'

'Why, run away with her, to be sure,' said the great banker, obviously having no idea what was in the young man's mind. 'Take her to Gretna Green.'

It must have seemed as near a blessing as Sarah Anne and John could expect and they went ahead with their plans. On the evening of Thursday, 16 May she persuaded her maid Mary Eldred, to administer a drug to her chaperone, who occupied the adjoining room in the tall house at Berkeley Square. Having made sure the chaperone was soundly asleep, Sarah Anne, with Mary's assistance, prepared to leave and in the small hours of Friday morning, she slipped out of the house, creeping silently past the footman who dozed in his high-backed chair by the front door. Mary Eldred had left a little earlier, carrying a few necessities for her mistress in a small parcel, and had a hackney carriage waiting at the corner of the street, for convention demanded that she must accompany her mistress. At once they drove off to the pre-arranged rendezvous where the Earl was eagerly awaiting them, with a post-chaise already harnessed-up, they all stepped inside and immediately the race to Gretna Green began. A journey of over 300 miles lay ahead of them.

Back in the house in Berkeley Square, the footman awoke to find the front door unlocked, and lost no time in rousing the household. Very quickly it was discovered that Sarah Anne and her maid were missing, a hue and cry was raised immediately, a post-chaise ordered and both Mr and Mrs Child set out in pursuit.

Possibly by accident, but more likely by design, it so happened that in the early morning of that Friday, the Hon Charles Grey, a friend of the Earl's and in command of a detachment of the King's Dragoon Guards, had his men out on exercise on the Great North Road. As the runaways' carriage came thundering along, Lord Westmorland put his head out of the window and called to his friend to help them by delaying Mr Child, who was close behind. Willingly Charles Grey arranged his Dragoons in such a way that it took a considerable time for the pursuers to pass. But before long the post-chaise had to be allowed through. Mr Child fumed and raged and urged his driver to whip up the horses and make up for lost time. When he was a little beyond Baldock, in Hertfordshire, he ordered his groom and another man to ride ahead and stop all carriages at the next turnpike. The groom, Richard Gillan, was mounted on Mr Child's favourite hunter which was a very fine animal. He rode fast, passing all the other traffic on the road and at last he caught up with the fugitives.

As the groom came galloping up alongside, Lord Westmorland looked out of the window of his post-chaise and drew his pistol, but he hesitated to fire. Sarah Anne recognised both rider and horse immediately and saw the danger.

'Shoot, my Lord,' she cried. 'Shoot.'

A shot rang out and the hunter fell dead although the rider was unharmed. Despite this Mr and Mrs Child continued the chase. The Earl had ordered horses to be in readiness all along the road and in the village

11

On Valentine's Day in 1985 there were fourteen weddings. One couple did not turn up, but it was still a record for one day. Nowadays 14 February is always requested by many more couples than can be fitted in. Those who are married on that day have sent in a postal application, carefully timed to arrive exactly three months earlier, on 14 November. They come from all over Great Britain and Ireland. No bookings can be taken more than three months in advance, and every year many couples are disappointed.

Some who especially want to be married on that day will make arrangements to go to one of the nearby Register Offices at Annan or Moffat, so they can easily visit the blacksmith's shops afterwards. Others determined to be married at Gretna, settle for the following day, or some other date.

---

of Shap, in Westmorland, he engaged every horse at the inn in a desperate attempt to delay pursuit.

Still Mr Child followed at great speed and through using great numbers of horses and by giving large sums of money to the post-boys, he managed not only to keep going but to gain considerable ground. At last he caught up with the runaways while they were changing horses at Hesketh-in-the-Forest, half way between Penrith and Carlisle. He jumped out in great fury and shot one of the leading horses belonging to the Earl's carriage. At the same time one of the Earl's servants ran behind Mr Child's carriage and, unobserved, cut the leather which attached the body of the carriage to the springs. The Earl, it was said, managed to proceed with only three instead of four horses. Mr Child, starting off again soon after, had not gone far before the body of his carriage fell upon its frame, which entirely stopped him, and at last he was compelled to abandon his pursuit.

John and Sarah Anne were driven on, still at top speed, to an ale-house by the river between Gretna and Annan, where the post-boy knew a wedding could quickly be arranged, and there they were married in the customary Scottish manner. Their marriage certificate was signed *John Brown*, which is known to be the pseudonym adopted in the early stage of the career of Joseph Pasley, a 'priest' of whom we shall hear more later. He claimed that he was paid a hundred guineas for the 'job'. Apparently there was no spare room at the inn for the newlyweds but the landlord woke up an elderly gentleman called Mr Henderson. This good-natured old man, who was in fact Lord Stormont's factor, agreed to move out of his room so that the young couple could have his bed for the night.

A few days later Lord Westmorland returned with his bride, the lovely young countess, to his seat at Apethorpe. Since the marriage was now *de facto*, Robert Child had little option but to accept it, and he gave his consent in order that the couple could be married according to the rites of the Church of England. This second ceremony was conducted by special licence at Apethorpe Hall on 5 June 1782 by the Vicar of Nassington.

Robert Child never forgave them. When, in an attempt to placate him, someone pointed out that at least his daughter had run away with a man of good blood, he answered savagely, 'Blood be damned! Robert Child's money – and he shall learn it – is better!' With that sentiment in mind, he made a new will with the purpose of cutting out the Westmorlands, then and for future generations. He bequeathed the residue of his enormous fortune, after the death of his wife, to the second son of Sarah Anne's future children, or failing that, to the eldest daughter, who should be called Sarah. Thus he ensured that, although his money would eventually pass to his grandchildren, it would never enrich an Earl of Westmorland. Two months later he died quite suddenly. He was only forty-three. It was said that his daughter's elopement had been such a blow to his hopes for his bank and for his name that he died of a broken heart.

The elopement and furious chase with its dramatic outcome, were not quickly forgotten. Sightseers even sought out the inn where the young couple were married and the bed in which they had consummated their vows was on show to visitors for several years afterwards.

The young couple prospered and in 1789, Lord Westmorland was sworn to the Privy Council and in the same year he became joint Postmaster-General. He had been educated at Charterhouse and Emmanuel College, Cambridge, where he had become a friend of William Pitt, a friendship which lasted throughout his life. Sarah Anne accompanied her husband when he was appointed Lord Lieutenant of Ireland in 1790. She bore six children and the eldest, John Fane, eventually succeeded his father to become 11th Earl of Westmorland but by the terms of Robert Child's will, he was barred from inheriting the wealth of the great banker. A second son was born in Dublin but he died soon after his birth, so it was their eldest daugher, Sarah Sophia, who became the sole heiress of her grandfather's immense fortune. Taking no chances, and to anticipate any legal quibbles that might arise, each new daughter had been christened with the gilded name of Sarah.

Sarah Anne was only twenty-eight when she died of a fever, in Dublin, on 9 November 1793. On reading of her death, Horace Walpole wrote:

Every Valentine's Day the press reporters flock to Gretna, seeking stories of romance. In 1985 they found William Armitage and Delia Moore, both in their mid-twenties, and both working as travel managers in Glasgow. They were taken quite by surprise at the publicity they walked into, especially as neither of them had even told their closest relatives they were getting married. Their photographs were already in the papers when they invited families and friends to a reception the next day.

Delia said, 'It was William's idea to be married in Gretna, he's the romantic.'

The oddest quote of that day came from Mr and Mrs Peter Horrocks, of Rowlands Castle, West Sussex, who claimed that their two pet dogs were acting as bridesmaids.

'A happy beauty, at the top of her prosperity.' Her body was sent back to England to be buried at Apethorpe but the weather was so appalling that the crossing took five days and the superstitious sailors wanted to throw the corpse into the sea. But Mary Eldred, who had gone with her mistress to Gretna Green, threw herself upon the coffin, and said that if it was thrown overboard, they must throw her with it.

In that same year Mrs Child, Robert's widow, also died and little Sarah Sophia, then only eight years old, inherited Child's Bank, the house in Berkeley Square and Osterley. Horace Walpole described this mansion in 1775 as 'the palace of palaces! but such expense! such taste! such profusion! ... there is a double portico that fills the space between the porticoes in front and as noble as the Propylaeum of Athens. There is a hall, library, breakfast room ... a gallery a hundred and thirty feet long ... and a drawing room worthy of Eve before the fall ... not to mention a kitchen garden that costs £1,400 a year and a menagerie of birds that come from a thousand islands'. Mrs Child, who had supervised the rebuilding of Osterley, was an accomplished artist and a lady of taste, moreover she not only had unlimited funds but the genius of Robert Adam at her command.

When Sarah Sophia was nineteen she married George Villiers, who the following year succeeded to the title of Earl of Jersey. He was an ardent horseman, famous on the turf as the breeder of three Derby winners, and referred to as 'not only one of the hardest, boldest and most judicious, but perhaps the most elegant rider to hounds the world ever saw'. With Sarah Sophia's great fortune they were both able to indulge their different interests.

14

The new Countess of Jersey became a leader of society and a political hostess, particularly enjoying the company of Benjamin Disraeli and Lord Byron. Her manner did not please everyone and some complained of her 'ebullience and coarseness of tone', which they found wearisome but she was a senior partner of Child's Bank and more often flattered for her wealth, her beauty and lively conversation. Before long she acquired the title 'Queen of Mayfair'; certainly she had great social power as a member of the committee who decided upon the right of admission to Almack's. For entry to this famous club, it was said you needed 'more qualifications than most people possess for admission to heaven'.

There were seven children from the marriage and the eldest son is said to have inherited the good looks of his grandfather, the Earl of Westmorland. For her daughters, Sarah Sophia worked like a beaver to procure good marriages. She stalked Prince Nicholas Esterhazy, son of the Austrian Ambassador, as a husband for her eldest daughter, also named Sarah. The hunt was long, the quarry sometimes disappearing into the wide plains of Hungary, but the match was at last achieved.

Her youngest daughter Lady Adela Coriande Maria Villiers was, however, of the same independent spirit as her grandmother, Sarah Anne Child, had been when it came to choosing a husband. She too eloped to Gretna Green. She set off one afternoon in the autumn of 1845 when the family were staying at their house in Brighton. It was at a time when her mother and two older sisters were away on a visit to the Duke and Duchess of Norfolk at Arundel Castle and only her father, Lord Jersey, remained in Brighton with Lady Adela.

'At dusk,' according to an article in *The Times* under the discreet heading 'Mysterious Disappearance of Lady Adela Villiers', 'Lady Adela was in the drawing-room with the earl and affectionately took leave of his lordship to, as she stated, go to the nursery, but at the dinner hour she was nowhere to be found . . . The young lady who is only seventeen years of age left her home on Wednesday afternoon at about quarter past five o'clock. It was expected that she had retired to her room with the intention of dressing for dinner, but not making her appearance at the table, on enquiries being instituted as to the cause of her absence, it was ascertained that her ladyship had some time previously passed through the lodge-gate with a small bundle in her hand . . .

'The distressing occurance has caused great excitement in the town. No cause whatever can be imagined as to what could induce the young lady to take such a step. No attendant has accompanied her ladyship and as far as the family can learn she had formed no attachment in opposition to the views of her parents.'

After taking leave of her father, Lady Adela had informed the servants that she was going to take a walk on the chain pier but having reached

In 1988 Valentine's Day fell on a Sunday – but it was a Leap Year, so 29 February took its place as the most popular date on the Gretna calendar.

Miss Bryden said, 'I could be booked up from 9 am to 5 pm but I have to keep it to a number we can cope with properly. Some people forget we have other things to deal with too – births and deaths, for instance. We have too many weddings at the moment, and I try to keep a balance.

'It's so difficult when people plead with you – "please, please put us in. We so want that date." I had one call from Ireland, and the girl went into hysterics because I dug my heels in and said, "no, we can't, we've got too many on that day already". Then her husband-to-be came on the phone and demanded to know who I was, and who was my superior because he was going to get in touch with him.' Miss Bryden told him, but added, 'You still will not be married on that day.' She had already offered them another date, and they came on that day and to her amazement they were 'as nice as ninepence'.

the Marine Parade, she called a fly and ordered the flyman to drive to the railway station. Here she was met by a tall gentleman, who held a handkerchief to his face to escape recognition as he bought two tickets for the last train to London.

Captain Charles Parke Ibbetson was in his late twenties and on leave from his regiment, the 11th Hussars, which was then based in Dublin. He had taken lodgings in Lower Rock Gardens, Brighton, and as *The Times* later reported 'There is little doubt that he used a portion of his leave in making arrangements for his flight with the fair fugitive as he was frequently seen looking towards East Lodge with an opera glass to his eye.' Immediately the news reached London, Lady Adela's brother, the Hon Captain Frederick Villiers, left town in pursuit. It was over sixty years since Sarah Anne Child had dashed northwards by post-chaise, and Lady Adela's journey and mode of conveyance was of a very different style. The London and Brighton Railway carried her and her beau to London and that same evening, just before nine o'clock, the couple were seen on the platform at Euston Square waiting for the train to York. Captain Ibbetson spoke to an official requesting 'To be accommodated with a coupé for himself and his fair companion, an act of attention which was immediately afforded.' A coupé was an end compartment of the carriage with seats on one side only. 'On arriving at

York station they breakfasted in the refreshment room, where the
elegant appearance and manner of Lady Adela was particularly remarked by several persons present.'

Captain Ibbetson had sent his private carriage ahead in charge of a
servant and this was loaded on a truck ready to be attached to the mail
train. At this stage, however, they were informed that 'the coupé in
which they had been comfortably ensconced throughout their journey
from Euston Square, would be no longer available to them. A suggestion
that they should jointly occupy the compartment of a first class carriage
in which two other persons were seated, met Captain Ibbetson's most
decided objection, and the gallant officer, in true military style, insisted
that a vacant carriage be afforded to him. This, after some little delay
and difficulty was accomplished, but the Captain's eloquence and
manner had such an effect on the servants of the railway that when
subsequently enquiries were made, the gallant officer's personal appearance was instantly remembered.

'The fugitives reached Carlisle shortly after one o'clock on Thursday
having thus run a distance of upwards of four hundred miles between
that hour and six o'clock the previous evening. Here they entered the
gallant Captain's carriage, and post horses having been furbished in a
very few moments, the party dashed through the fine old city en route
for the border.'

At Gretna Hall, John Linton, landlord and 'priest' was presiding at a
luncheon, the guests at which consisted chiefly of a party of engineers
planning an extension to the railway line. A message was sent to 'mine
host' that a lady and gentleman had just arrived from London and were
awaiting his services in the saloon upstairs. He immediately vacated his
post at the head of the table withdrew briefly and returned 'attired in full
canonicals'.

'The first procedure was to obtain the names of both parties, with a
proper description of their respective residences. Here for an instant a
difficulty was apprehended. Lady Adela confessed that at the moment
she could only recollect three of her Christian names, though she
believed she had more. Our host soon calmed her ladyship's misgivings

17

by declaring that all the names were not necessary, instancing a case where the same omission had been declared valid – that of the Prince de Capua, who, possessing a string of something like sixteen names, when asked to state them at Gretna, could only recollect about one half the number.'

The names obtained, witnesses were called, one of whom was Mrs Linton and the other one of the Carlisle postillions. 'The ceremony commenced by a declaration on the part of both her ladyship and the gallant officer, to the effect that they were single persons, and that they had come to Gretna freely and willingly, of their own accord and without force.

'The gallant Captain next took the left hand of his fair companion and having placed the ring thereon, mine host joined their hands together and declared the parties man and wife in the following terms – "Forasmuch as this man and this woman have consented together before God and these people to be man and wife by receiving this ring, I hereby declare them to be such in the presence of God and these witnesses."

'The marriage was then recorded in the usual manner upon a printed form prepared for the purpose. At four o'clock, the best horses the stable afforded were put to the carriage and the Captain having, with a bounteous hand, satisfied all claims upon his purse, handed his youthful bride to her seat and springing into the carriage himself, the happy pair drove off together in the direction of Edinburgh. They reached Langholm, a distance of sixteen miles, and the first stage upon the old road to Edinburgh, before six o'clock. Relays of horses were here provided at the Crown Inn and our travellers again proceeded onwards, arriving at about eight o'clock at Moss Paul, a lone hostelrie, the property of the Duke of Buccleuch, situated about midway between Gretna and Hawick. At this place they rested for the night, intending to proceed early the next morning on their way to Edinburgh. We believe they are now staying in that city.'

Captain Frederick Villiers, in pursuit, had a much less successful trip. He was late from the start, leaving London on Thursday afternoon by the four o'clock express. He changed at Wolverton in Buckinghamshire and boarded the train to York. There he tried to 'procure a special engine but could not obtain one and he was perforce compelled to await the arrival of the nine pm London mail before he could move a mile further northward.' He was over a day late in reaching Gretna Green, so simply 'procured a copy of the marriage certificate, communicated the result by letter to his noble parents and returned to town'.

Sarah Sophia, who had gained such an enormous fortune as a result of her own mother's elopement, was shocked and distraught when Adela disappeared, and furious over the scandal she caused. Again, however, once the step had irrevocably been made, Adela's parents could do nothing but make a virtue out of necessity and with their consent the couple went through a second wedding ceremony at a fashionable London church.

For the general public such spirited escapades built up the reputation of Gretna Green. Had Sarah Anne Child been born a generation or so earlier she would not have needed to undertake that long journey to Scotland and her marriage to the handsome young Earl of Westmorland could have been conducted within walking distance of her London home. It was the Marriage Act of 1754 which changed that and by so doing, sent thousands of couples travelling northwards over the border.

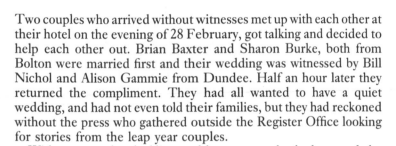

Two couples who arrived without witnesses met up with each other at their hotel on the evening of 28 February, got talking and decided to help each other out. Brian Baxter and Sharon Burke, both from Bolton were married first and their wedding was witnessed by Bill Nichol and Alison Gammie from Dundee. Half an hour later they returned the compliment. They had all wanted to have a quiet wedding, and had not even told their families, but they had reckoned without the press who gathered outside the Register Office looking for stories from the leap year couples.

With a merry laugh Alison told reporters she had popped the question to Brian on the previous leap year day, but it had taken four years to get him to the Register Office.

CHAPTER THREE

# Why Gretna?

In the British Isles laws and customs concerning marriage have been many and varied, and Scotland had, and still has, many differences from England in this respect. In days gone by this was particularly so in the border districts, and strangest of all was that at Langholm in Dumfriesshire, a few miles north of Gretna. There on a piece of flat pasture where the waters of the Black and the White Esk meet, a Handfasting Fair used to be held every August until the eighteenth century. As well as the usual buying and selling and all the robust gaiety of the fair, it was an opportunity for couples to enter a year's trial marriage.

On the greensward, beside the burbling stream, a lover and his lass could clasp hands and promise to remain faithful to each other for the coming twelve months. It was as simple as that and they were bound for only one year; when fairtime came again the choice had to be made definitely. Those that decided to remain together would seek out the 'wandering Friar' and bind themselves in the usual marriage ceremony. Couples who wished to relinquish their vow parted, under no obligation or disgrace, with the single proviso that if there was a child, it became the responsibility of whichever parent had opted out of the union.

Perhaps this old custom was brought to Scotland by the Romans for under their law, marriage was a civil contract and had no religious significance. It was based only on the consent of both parties and could be easily dissolved. There was also a Roman custom that if a woman lived with a man for a year, with the permission of her parents or guardians and without being absent for three nights, she became his wife.

Equally it might have derived from an ancient Celtic rite. In that distant era, contracts of various kinds, including marriages, were sealed by both parties clasping hands through a hole in a large stone. In the Orkneys a relic of this is known as Odin's Stone.

When ventriloquist Neville King married Joan Lambert, the dancer, their friend, Ken Dodd went along too, and took Miss Bryden completely by surprise. 'I had no idea he was coming. I never know who it will be until they step through that door. It really was quite a day.'

Having the Squire of Knotty Ash at a Gretna wedding made the headlines in October 1986, and everyone was delighted. The bride arrived at the Register Office in a horse and carriage driven by a local farmer, Bert Edgar, while his grand-daughter, Kerry, played the role of 'footman'. A crowd quickly gathered to see Joan arrive, wearing a beautiful ivory wedding gown with ruched neckline. A swish of her skirts revealed the traditional blue garter, which delighted the male onlookers.

All the chairs had to be taken out of the tiny wedding room to accommodate the 40 guests, who had to stand during the ceremony. Ken Dodd maintained a very low profile while the serious part of the ceremony was undertaken – but afterwards everyone was treated to a hilarious comedy act. The ventriloquist groom threw his voice around, making a dog bark from behind one of Miss Bryden's pot plants, shouts appeared to come from outside, and he carried on a crazy two-way conversation into the phone.

Miss Bryden may not have known the celebrities would be there but Border Television did, and when they and the photographers took the wedding pictures, Neville, far from trying to look his best, used his expertise as a girner to twist his rubber-like features into comical grimaces.

Having fun, but not making a mock of their wedding, the couple went to All Saints Episcopal Church, where the Rev Vincent Kendall blessed their union. Then they went to the Gretna Hall Blacksmith's Shop for the anvil marriage ceremony, and the party put on an act as good as any television comedy, with Ken Dodd wielding the shotgun, and Neville screaming in mock pain as Jim Jackson clanged the hammer down on the anvil.

Pat Bryden said, 'It was a wonderful wedding. There were some really funny moments after the ceremony.' By chance it coincided with her fortieth anniversary in the Register Office, and her pleasure was completed when Fiona Armstrong from Border Television presented her with a bouquet of flowers.

Certainly the Scottish borderland was remote and inaccessible in the Middle Ages and cut off from the south by the great rivers of the Tweed and the Solway Firth. The religious affairs of this wild area were administered by friars from the priories of Melrose and Jedburgh, who were often spoken of as 'book-a-besoms' because they carried their mass book in the folds of their habits, to keep it safe, while leaving the monk's hands free to guide his pony or carry his staff. They attended all the local fairs, and on their journeying they performed ceremonies of baptism, marriage or said prayers for the dead.

At that time there was no need for a religious, or even a civil ceremony for a wedding at Langholm, or anywhere else in Scotland – or indeed in England either. All that was necessary was for a declaration to be made by both parties before two witnesses and the union was legal and binding. Although in most cases some sort of certificate or 'marriage line' was given, there was no need for any written record to be kept and this haphazard state of affairs led to considerable legal difficulties. In England this was amended by Lord Hardwicke's Marriage Act of 1754 but in Scotland 'irregular' marriages remained within the law until 1940. Before then there was no simple answer to the problem of defining what was and what was not a marriage. The Church had attempted to regularise the situation by declaring that all marriages had to be performed by the clergy in a church, but in law there was nothing that decreed this to be so.

Although this declaration before two witnesses was all that was necessary, most people found it hard to believe that this would be really and truly binding. As time went by, brides and grooms increasingly wanted some sort of ceremony, however brief, and believed that their vows should be made before a priest or someone they felt was vested with the right authority. An orthodox priest could and would only perform marriages under the rules of the Church but there were certain parishes that lay outside that jurisdiction. In London such an area lay around the Fleet Prison, Mayfair, the King's Bench Prison, the Mint and the Savoy. It was here, therefore, that a 'trade' in marriages sprang up, the most notorious of all was the Fleet Prison and its surrounding streets. There was no need for banns to be read or a licence to be bought, you could be married immediately. There were touts who accosted every couple in the street.

'Do you wish to be married?' one would ask. 'Just step inside and I'll do the job for you.'

Or: 'I can take you to a good parson.'

'That fellow will take you to a peddling alehouse,' a rival tout would declare. 'Come to my man – he's a real Oxford and Cambridge professor.'

Some of the marriages were conducted in the chapel of the prison itself where many of the inmates, who included parsons, were debtors. As the trade grew marriages were performed in a variety of places – in the back rooms of inns, in shops or in brothels, in the pastrycooks, the shoemakers, in a cellar under the Fountain Inn, or anywhere you paid the parson to go. There were no restrictions on hours and many marriages are recorded as taking place around midnight. Representatives of all levels of society made use of these clandestine ceremonies for all sorts of reasons, as extracts from the old registers show:

*June 10th 1729. John Nelson of ye parish of St. George, Hanover. Bachelor and gardener to Mary Barns of the same address, spinster. Certificate dated 5th November 1727 to please their parents.*

*Nov 5th 1742 – was married Benjamin Richards of the parish of St. Martin in the Fields, bachelor and Judith Lance, of the same address spinster. At the Bull and Garter. They gave a guinea for the marriage to be antedated to 11th March in the same year and were put in the register accordingly there being a vacancy in the book suitable at the time.*

*Nov 6th 1735. John Fletcher, a butcher of St. Clements's Danes and Hannah Neelor of St. Andrews, Holbourne, bachelor and spinster. This couple had co-habited many years but upon a small legacy being left they thought it proper to marry.*

Another couple 'wanted eighteen years back.'

On at least one occasion 'the woman ran across Ludgate Hill in her shift'. This was because there was a belief that a man was not liable for the bride's debts, if he took her in no other apparel than her shift. Despite her valiant effort unfortunately this was never true.

Most parsons kept a separate book for the purpose of recording marriages which were desired to be kept secret. Nearly all the contracting parties in this book were of a superior station in life, being designated as gent and spinster.

*Sept 8th. Edward Emmet, gent of Barking in Essex to Hannah Bowle at the Castle Tavern, Paternoster Row, 'was to be secret for a month'.*

In a great many instances the parties refused to tell their surnames.

*March ye 4th 1740 William          and Sarah          . He dressed in a gold waistcoat like an officer, she a beautiful young lady with two fine diamond rings and a black high crown hat and very well dressed. They were married at Boyces.*

*September 11th 1745 Edward          and Elizabeth
were married and would not let me know their names, ye man said he was a
weaver and lived in Bandyleg Walk in the borough.*

*May 24th 1742 – a soldier brought a barber to the Cock who said his name
was James – was in part married to Elizabeth. They said they were married
enough and left without even those brief formalities being completed.*

There were some odd clients!

*May 20th 1737. John Smith gent of St James, Westminster, bachelor and
Elizabeth Huthall of St Giles, spinster, at Wilsons. By ye opinion after
matrimony my Clerk judged they were both women. If ye person by name John
Smith be a man he is a little, short fair thin man not above five foot. After
marriage I almost could prove them both women, the one dressed as a man,
thin, pale face, and wrinkled chin.*

*Oct 1st 1747 – John Ferren, Gent of St Andrew's Holborn and Deborah
Nolan of the same address, spinster. The supposed John Ferren was discovered
after ye ceremonie were over to be in person a woman.*

*July 22nd 1728 Josiah Welsh, a cordwainer and Elizabeth Cutchey of St
Giles, Cambridge. Widower and spinster – brought by Mr Ralf and Mr
Hargrove of the Guards, who paid me two guineas to provide a husband for
Madame and defray all the subsequent charges of the wedding.*

*December 11th 1727 – Walter Janes, cordwainer of St Martin's Ludgate and
Mary Spreadborough of St Giles in the Fields. Widower and spinster. The
man had five shillings for marrying her. N.B. the above person married in
common.*

The parson was clearly aware that he was a bigamist. Welsh, alias Janes
and other names, married four women in fourteen months, each time
changing his name. The object of the bride paying for a husband, or in
getting another woman to pose as such, was either to enable her to plead
coverture to an action for debt, or to give her a certificate to show in case of
being pregnant. In either case of course, the 'husband' would make sure
he was untraceable. Another such bridegroom is marked 'paid for his
trouble'. Perhaps some spirit of Christianity shows through occasionally.

*July 22nd 1728 Nicholas Richardson, invalid soldier in Chelsea Hospital
and Judith Taylor of Chelsea. Widower and widow. Married at Chidleys. I
gave a certificate and was paid with a promise.*

There were other ways of augmenting the priest's income.

*December 10th 1728, William Salkeld, marriner and Mary Jones, both of St Andrews, Holborn. They were married at twelve at night and lay all night in bed in my house, for which had one shilling and sixpence more — already paid for the wedding sixteen shillings.*

*April 9th 1727 Edmund David, a Hatter of St George's, Bloomsbury and Mary Sprigg Martin of St Giles in the Fields. This couple were bedded about six minutes and paid only five shillings per total.*

Some couples were brought by the Overseers of the Poor.

*July 22nd 1741, Paid three shillings. A parish wedding and the people being pretty remarkable. I believe there was a mob of 300 people after them. The bridegroom was a miserable blind youth, known by the name of Ambrose Tally, who plays the violin in Moorfields.*

The churchwardens of one city parish bribed the couple to marry by giving the bride forty shillings and paying the expense of a Fleet wedding in order to shift them off their own books and settle them in the neighbouring parish of Shoreditch. Little was left of the bride's parish 'fortune' by the next day, as they were followed by a 'great many poor wretches', invited and uninvited, who helped them to celebrate.

*August 22nd 1744 Robert Parker, labourer of Yoel in Surrey and Hannah Horton of the same address. Bachelor and spinster, at the Shepherd and Goat. The officers of the Parish took the fellow up by warrant to force him to marry her — vile behaved.*

*May 2nd John Harrowson of the Duke Man o' War, and Susannah Lawson. This said Harrowson swore most bitterly and was pleased to say that he was fully determined to kill the Minister that married him. He came from Gravesend and was sober.*

*1735. Yesterday morning an odd affair happened. A young man and woman — country people and very well dressed, came to be married, but before the minister had half performed the ceremony the woman was delivered of a daughter. This poor girl, though literally born in wedlock, seems to be somewhat more than half a bastard!*

*June 11th 1727 William Whittingham, watchmaker and Rachel Babington, both of St Olaves, Silver Street. Rachel was the prettiest woman I ever saw.*

*August 12th 1729 Abraham Wells, a butcher of the parish of Tottenham in Middlesex and Susannah Hewitt of Enfield, widower and widow. N.B. 28th April 1736 Mrs Wells came and ernestly entreated me to erase the marriage out of the book, for that her husband had beat and abused her in barbarous manner and she had much rather be esteemed his whore that she might have a proper recourse of Law against him. I made her believe I did so for which I had half a guinea and she at the same time delivered me up her Certificate. No person present according to her desire.*

*August 29th 1729. John Wills, distiller of St Dunstan's in the East and Mary Mackarty of St Andrew's Holborn. Widower and widow. Two most notorious thieves.*

At least once the Minister was threatened.

*Feb 25th Robert Taylor and Margaret                came into my apartment and behaved very rudely, swore sadly, obliged me to marry them for what they pleased to pay me, for fear of my life, late at night, by the names above mentioned.*

By the early eighteenth century there were as many as sixty marriage houses near the Fleet Prison, many symbolised by the hanging sign of two crossed hands. There are hundreds of registers and pocket books containing almost two hundred thousand marriages and some baptisms, most of which are now held by Somerset House in London. The names of about sixty parsons are known and there may have been more. The Church of England Marriage Service was generally used, though it was often slightly curtailed. Undoubtedly most of these unions were normal, honest love matches but the looseness of the system encouraged abuse by a growing proportion of fortune-hunters and bigamists, while the corrupt and greedy parsons could easily be bribed to forge documents, change dates or perjure themselves when cases came to law. It has been estimated that in the late seventeenth and early eighteenth centuries not much more than half the population were being married strictly according to the rules of the Church, and of those that were, a great many had already entered into full sexual relationships. Many of the poor never married at all but lived in a form of concubinage, while the upper classes and prosperous bourgeoisie normally evaded all canonical restrictions on time and place by obtaining a special licence.

The aristocracy and gentry were particularly disturbed by this hopeless legal tangle because it often affected the inheritance of their property. They were especially worried by the ease with which penniless adventurers could entice and seduce their daughters and heiresses and

A Jewish couple made the long journey from Israel to Gretna. Miss Bryden remembered them specially because they had made so many phone calls to make sure everything was in order, and they brought along some friends from Holland as witnesses. Although they were both Jewish they weren't of the same tribe and their families didn't approve.

irrevocably marry them, without parental knowledge or consent, at any place or at any hour of the day or night. It was also possible for a rebellious daughter to refuse to marry the man of her father's choice by claiming that she had already entered into a contract at the Fleet. Such a claim, true or false, could be supported by bribed witnesses so that it was impossible to disprove, and no legitimate parson would perform the nuptial rites if there was a possibility it might make the bride a bigamist.

After the passing of the Marriage Act, such doubts were covered by the publishing of the Banns of Marriage – 'If any of you know cause or just impediment, why these two persons should not be joined together in holy matrimony, ye are to declare it.' It was the last of several attempts made by the House of Lords to introduce control over clandestine marriages, since all previous attempts had been defeated by the Commons, and though this Act was eventually passed, it had a stormy passage through Parliament.

The Act laid down that:

1 Only church weddings and not verbal spousals should be legally binding.
2 All church marriages had to be entered in the Parish Register, signed by both parties.
3 All marriages which occurred at times or in places defined as illegal by the 1604 Canons were declared invalid.
4 No marriage of persons under twenty-one was valid without the consent of parents or guardians.
5 The above laws were to be enforced by the secular courts, which could impose up to fourteen years transportation on clergymen who disobeyed the law.

The main argument against the Bill was that it would give the aristocracy such a hold over their children that they would be able to keep their heiresses exclusively for marriage within their own ranks, and that this would create a closed and increasingly wealthy caste in society. Riches, it was argued, should be made to circulate through certain marriages to commoners. The health of the aristocracy might even be in danger – 'what sort of breed their offspring will be we may easily judge, if the gout, the gravel, the pox and madness are always wed together'. Besides it was the natural right of minors to marry whom they pleased, rather than be bullied into arranged and loveless marriages. Finally, it was feared that the Bill would make marriage both difficult and expensive for the poor, bringing about an increase in concubinage, bastardy and infanticide.

One of those most strenuously opposed to the Bill was the Hon Henry Fox, who ten years earlier had secretly been married by a Fleet parson to Lady Georgina Caroline Lennox. Her parents, the Duke and Duchess of Richmond, had refused their consent and the wedding had caused a great stir in London society. In his early years, Henry Fox had recklessly indulged in gambling and other extravagances so that he had soon squandered the greater part of his own fortune and had had to go abroad. With such a reputation and being much older than Lady Georgina, it was not surprising the Duke and Duchess had doubted his suitability as a match for their daughter. Nevertheless the marriage was a very happy one and the couple had four sons. Several years later Lady Georgina's parents were reconciled to their daughter.

Henry Pelham, the Prime Minister in 1754, had cause to support the Bill however. In the summer of 1735 his sister Miss Pelham, who was as beautiful as she was rich and well-born, was staying in Ranelagh Gardens, Chelsea, and there became acquainted with a handsome young gentleman. They danced and talked and fell in love. He professed to be a gentleman of fortune and before long proposed marriage, sweeping the young lady off her feet. But both knew their union would meet with strenuous objections from her family so they arranged to go to the Fleet to be wed. There, they were conducted to a parson but by chance they were seen by a gentleman who knew Miss Pelham. He also recognised her lover as a notorious highwayman whose name was Jack Freeland, but who also had numerous aliases. The gentleman stopped the marriage, had the highwayman arrested and carried the tidings to her brother.

The Act finally came into force on 26 March 1754 and Fleet marriages went on till the very last moment. In one register alone there is a list of 217 weddings celebrated on 25 March. Twenty years later a woman wrote to *The Lady's Magazine* alleging that 'no law was ever made that has occasioned so many broken hearts, unhappy lives and accumulated distress as this has'.

It remained basically unchanged until 1970 and it was a powerful piece of restrictive legislation. But young love is not easy to suppress and those determined to marry to please themselves began to search for a way out. The law of Scotland had not been changed, and north of the border anyone could still be married in the old way, almost instantly and without parental consent. Gradually this information seeped southwards – and the first village over the border on the main road from London, through Carlisle, was Gretna Green.

*Gretna Green* gets a little publicity on the waterways of Holland, for one couple who were married in the Scottish village named their barge after it.

CHAPTER FOUR

# The Rush Begins

The first rush of romantic couples to Gretna Green began in the 1770s. It increased enormously as transport was improved by the building of turnpike roads and the setting up of regular coach runs to the north. Scotland was not the only haven for runaways, some couples went to the Isle of Man and others to the Channel Islands since neither of those places was affected by Lord Hardwicke's Act. But before long the Tynwald brought the marriage law of the Isle of Man in line with England, while in those days, the Channel Islands were difficult to reach.

At Gretna the marriage trade just grew and grew. One of the parsons from the Fleet prison, having been forced to shut his marriage shop there, settled his debts and advertised his removal to Gretna. It was most probably this parson who introduced the English Church formula to the Scottish irregular wedding although it was a much shortened version, and could be adapted at will to suit the occasion. It was soon adopted by all the 'priests'.

Marriages were performed in a great many places in the border region, but nowhere were there as many as in Gretna and its immediate environs. Before the making of the turnpike to Gretna in 1777, communication was often made by boat or by fording the Solway. This could be a hazardous journey, even for those who knew the countryside.

One of the earliest recorded stories is that of Jean Scott, the daughter of a yeoman farmer, whose ancestors had farmed land in Wetheral, in Cumberland, for generations. Jean fell in love with a handsome young man called John Edgar. Whether he was one of her father's workmen or simply a poor young countryman from the nearby village, is not known but certainly his position in the social scale was much lower than hers. Jean has been described as the 'winsomest wench in all Cumberland' and her father planned to make an excellent match for her but she was determined to marry no one but John.

It was in 1771 that the couple planned their elopement. Jean managed to slip out of the farmhouse without being seen, lifted her long skirts and ran to the place where John was waiting for her. He had horses saddled and together they rode for the border. As luck would have it, it was not long before Mr Scott discovered that his daughter had gone – he may well have suspected that she might attempt to run away. The labourers in those days lived on the farm and the furious father quickly roused his men and set out in pursuit. The lovers headed for the ford across the Solway, their nearest route into Scotland, but Mr Scott had the advantage of knowing the countryside better than they did and he took a short-cut, thus managing to get ahead of them on the road. Jean and John, however, had friends in the area and somehow the message was got to them that they had been outflanked. Their only hope was to turn westwards and try to get a boat across the water.

Knowing that Jean's father would not be far behind, they spurred their horses on and came at last to the little village of Burgh-by-Sands, on the Solway Firth. The estuary stretching between England and Scotland is some three miles wide at this point, it was growing dark and the tide was running full, so John found some boatmen, but conditions were bad and the men were reluctant to put out. The lovers were desperate. They offered more money, and Jean told their story; a group of daring young mariners agreed to attempt the crossing. Their crew consisted of brave but lawless young seamen who thought nothing of poaching for salmon and who had smuggled many a keg of brandy into the country. They clambered into the small open boat.

The tide rushed along with the speed of a river in full spate, hissing and swirling to the very end of the Firth. It swept angrily into creeks and channels and bit into the treacherous sandbanks, crashing them down into the seething waters. The little rowing boat was pushed off, its crew straining at the oars to keep it on course, and Jean and John crouched together in the stern. They had scarcely left the shore when Mr Scott rode up with his men.

'A boat. A boat!' he demanded.

No one would help him. The tide was raging more furiously than ever, darkness deepening with every moment. The local boatmen knew only too well the dangers of the rushing waters of the Solway – and they knew too of the young lovers who had set out only minutes before. No amount of money that Mr Scott offered would tempt any of them to set out. Angrily he pushed past the locals and commanded his men to take and launch the first boat they came to. Jean looked back and saw the boat with her father and his men leave the shore. She and John huddled together as wave after wave broke over the rowing boat, and their brave oarsmen pulled their hardest. All of them were drenched to the skin and the boat was carried

On 23 July 1986, while most of the country watched the wedding of Prince Andrew and Sarah Ferguson, business went on as usual in the Register Offices of Scotland. Eight couples were married that day in Gretna, making it the most important day in their lives, too. When Kenneth Irwin and Elaine Maughan made their wedding arrangements they had no idea they would be sharing it with the royal couple. They travelled over one hundred miles from Wishaw, to the village of romance.

Another couple, from Lanarkshire, were Patricia Houston and Marshall Muir, whose home was in Shotts. They hadn't wanted the fuss of a big wedding, and kept their visit a secret. But someone evidently found out, for shortly after they left the Register Office a bouquet of flowers arrived for them.

Earlier in the week Sarah Ferguson and Prince Andrew were interviewed on television, and Sarah had commented that she would happily have married her Prince at Gretna Green! Pat Bryden said, with a smile, that she would have been delighted to officiate for them.

downstream towards the open sea as the tide began to ebb. They lost sight of Mr Scott's boat. His men were not seamen and almost immediately after it was launched a wave overturned the boat and threw all the pursuing party into the water. One man was caught in an undercurrent and drowned.

Jean and John knew nothing of this, their hopes were set on reaching the opposite shore safely. Their boatmen were strong, skilful and they knew the treacherous waters of the Solway well. Steadfastly they rowed on until they landed at the little fishing hamlet of Browhouses which was no more than a cluster of cottages. It was late at night and they were two miles west of Gretna. One of the boatmen knocked on the door of a cottage where some friends of his lived, and called them up from their beds. They blew up the embers of the peat fire and soon all were being dried and warmed by its glow. Jean and John still feared that Mr Scott might be following, and at first light the next morning they walked to Gretna Green. The first house they would come to belonged to Joseph Pasley. He became one of the principal figures in the Gretna story, and over the years he married many couples, but it is probable that Jean Scott and John Edgar were among the first of his 'clients'.

Among the brides who ran away to Gretna were some of the loveliest, richest and most aristocratic young ladies of England – and from Europe and other parts of the world also. Their amorous adventures continually kept the border village in the news.

When in 1811 Elizabeth Sophia, daughter of Sir Edward Nightingale, eloped with Charles Ewan Law, it was again a case of history repeating itself. Her parents had themselves run away to a Gretna wedding at the end of the eighteenth century. Elizabeth and Charles apparently settled down to a long and happy life, they had three children and their son succeeded his uncle and became Lord Ellenborough.

Less than a month after that elopement Lady Mary Beauclerk, daughter of the Duke of St Albans, ran away with George William, Lord Deerhurst, who was a widower with two small children and heir to the Earl of Coventry. Perhaps this did not surprise 'the ton' too much. Lady Mary, a descendent of King Charles II and Nell Gwynn, had shocked society before. She had inherited an estate of £100,000 when she was only ten years old and when she was sixteen she absolutely scandalised society by walking unchaperoned in the park with a handsome young lieutenant. What was even worse, she insisted on riding astride when all demure and well-bred young ladies rode side-saddle! She has been described as beautiful, very petite, brisk, lively and agreeable, with eyes that were 'brilliant, gentle and magnificent'. The smallness of her hands and feet were so famous that they were reproduced in marble by Pizzi, the notable Italian sculptor. But unfortunately, the union was not a happy one. After the birth of their second child, Mary left her husband and went to live in Rome where she continued to scandalise *le monde*.

Prince Charles, a member of the Italian royal family and brother of King Ferdinand of Naples, was married at Gretna Hall on 7 May 1836. His bride was a lovely Irish girl, Penelope Smyth, and this was their fourth wedding ceremony. In less than three months they were married five times, each time in a different country.

Penelope was the daughter of Mr Grice Smyth of Ballynatray, County Waterford, in Ireland. She was the second daughter of a family of eight children and at the time of her meeting with the Prince, she was living in an ordinary English middle-class house on the edge of Exeter. She was very pretty and virtuous, and the Prince fell so desperately in love with her that he was willing to renounce his right of succession to the throne of Italy to marry her. But even then, being a prince of the blood royal, he was not permitted to wed without the permission of his brother the king, and this was withheld.

Despite this, the loving couple set off for Rome in February 1836 where they sought an audience with the Pope and asked for his sanction to their union. Evidently this was granted, for they went through a private ceremony of marriage at the royal villa of Marlia, near Lucca, which at that time was an independent republic. They were married for a second time in Madrid and again in Rome by Cardinal Wold, but even then the validity of these three marriages remained in doubt. They went to London where on 16 April they attended a reception given by His Majesty King William IV. Then, having heard of the strength of Scottish law on the subject of marriage, off the pair went to Gretna. They were married at Gretna Hall and the entry in the marriage register reads 'Carlo Ferdinando Borbone, Principe de Capua from the Parish of Castello Nuovo, County – and state de Napoli de Italia to Penelope Carolina Smyth from the Parish of Temple Michael, County Waterford, Ireland'.

Still their doubts had not been properly settled, and almost immediately after they made an application to the Court of Faculties at Doctor's Commons, the college of civil law in London. This was for a licence to solemnise, or re-solemnise, the marriage, according to the forms of the Church of England. The Prince's brother, King Ferdinand, slapped a *caveat* on this through his Sicilian envoy which attempted to prevent the ceremony on the grounds that the Prince and the lady had eloped from Naples. The proctor for King Ferdinand's minister insisted that, by decree of the Sicilian kingdom, no valid marriage could be contracted by a Prince of the blood royal, without the consent of the reigning sovereign. The licence was refused, but the banns were afterwards published in the orthodox way, and although the couple had been forbidden to marry by the King, no just cause to prevent the marriage could legally be shown. So, in the fashionable church of St George's, Hanover Square, London, they were married for the fifth time.

After this King Ferdinand and his family could no longer dispute the fact that the Prince and his bride had satisfied the legal requirements of five European countries. Yet Penelope was never fully accepted by them. She was relegated to the position of a morganatic wife, never treated as royalty and allowed no share in the Prince's official status. She died in 1882.

On 20 May 1840 a gallant horseman, Lord Archibald Drumlanrig, came riding into Gretna with his lady seated before him. He was then aged twenty-two, and was the son and heir of the Marquess of Queensberry. His lady's name was Caroline Clayton and she was the daughter of a general who thought her too young to know her own mind, but Lord Archibald came of a line that never brooked refusal and he carried her off to Gretna Hall.

A few years after their elopement, one of the Drumlanrig grooms ran away with one of the maids. Determined on speed, he chose his master's most valuable hunter to ride upon. But too excited to be careful, the groom brought back the horse lame and had no option but to confess what he had done. His lord was furious. The young couple expected instant dismissal but his wife heard of the episode and intervened.

'Why Archie!' she exclaimed, 'would you have minded how many horses were lamed when you eloped with me?'

He was then restored to good humour and the servants kept their positions. Lady Caroline was a lady of strong character and independent thought. She was a warm advocate of Home Rule for Ireland and wrote several pamphlets, chiefly of a religious nature. Lord Drumlanrig succeeded his father in 1856 but two years later he was killed when rabbit-shooting on their estate of Kinmount. The couple had only one son, born in 1844, who later became renowned as the patron of boxing.

On Saturday 10 October, 1846 another aristocratic elopement hit the headlines. 'Elopement in High Life' proclaimed the *Gloucester Journal.* 'The Ladies Blanche and Rose Somerset, with their youthful sisters, have been staying at Badminton for some days, during the absence of their parents, who have been on a visit to Sir Charles Morgan at Tredegar. On Friday evening the family retired to rest at the usual hour. Nothing had occurred up to this time to excite the slightest suspicion of the intention of the Lady Rose to quit her home, but at seven o'clock on Saturday morning, when the attendants, as usual, went upstairs to call her ladyship, she was not to be found, but there was a letter addressed to her noble parents. This occasioned some suspicion and an open window, looking from one of the drawing rooms on to the lawn, increased this feeling, and further enquiries placed the fact of her departure beyond a doubt.'

The Duke and Duchess were sent for immediately and the letter 'disclosed to whose protection their daughter had resigned herself'. The Lady Rose and Captain Francis Lovell arrived at Gloucester at five o'clock on Saturday morning and drove to the railway station in a coach and four. 'At the station a special train, which had previously been ordered to be in readiness as early as three o'clock, was waiting to receive them, and they at once steamed away to Birmingham.' A special train could be hired for the price of eight first class tickets at this time.

Francis Lovell was obviously thought to be socially inferior to the Lady Rose even though 'the gallant captain' was a 'member of a respected family, highly esteemed in his own circle and in the same regiment as the Marquess of Worcester'. Moreover, she was only seventeen, while it was perceived that 'from forty to forty-five summers have passed over his head ... the gallant captain has moreover lost his left arm, from the bursting of his gun whilst pigeon shooting some few years since. On that occasion, the manly and soldier-like firmness with which he endured the pain of his severe wound and his unflinching demeanour whilst the amputation proceeded were as much admired as his sad misfortune was lamented. Notwithstanding the loss of his bridle arm, he had been allowed to continue to hold his commission.'

Captain Lovell had obtained leave from his regiment, the 1st Life Guards, who were stationed at Windsor. He was married to the Lady Rose at Gretna Hall.

'Do you ken John Peel with his coat so gay?' The huntsman, immortalised by the ballad, was himself married at Gretna to 'bonny Mary White'. The banns for their wedding had been put up in Caldbeck Parish Church but Mr White objected on the grounds that his daughter was far too young. Not to be thwarted, Mary climbed out of her bedroom window, dropped into the arms of her dashing young huntsman and rode with him over the border. Like many another couple they later received a blessing on their marriage in their own church.

Three Lord Chancellors of England contracted 'irregular' marriages in Scotland, though only one of them was at Gretna. The first was John Scott, later Lord Eldon. He was born in Love Lane, Newcastle, in 1751, the son of a prosperous coal-fitter and he was educated at the Royal Free Grammar School and at University College, Oxford. When he was about twenty years old, while on a visit to Sedgefield in South Durham, he attended the fine old Gothic church there and noticed a very pretty girl. She was about eighteen, slight of figure with dark brown hair that streamed in ringlets down her neck and she was said to have features of exquisite perfection. Her name was Elizabeth Surtees and he fell deeply in love.

John Scott at that time was an impoverished college tutor, while Elizabeth's father, Aubone Surtees, was a banker in Newcastle. He was looking for a more promising husband for his daughter and did all he could to prevent their meeting. He sent Bessy to stay with her uncle in the south of England but the lovers contrived to meet often, and they wrote to each other regularly. The Surtees lived in a large, old-fashioned house, one of a row in a street called Sandhill. On the ground floor was the shop and warehouse of a clothier which was not in any way connected with the house, but it helped John Scott to work out a plan for the elopement. He made friends with one of the apprentices, a young man named Wilkinson, and persuaded him to hide a ladder on the clothier's premises. He chose a time when Bessy's older brother was away for a few days and on the night of Wednesday, 18 November 1772, John set the ladder against a first floor window and Bessy climbed down. They travelled overnight by coach across the border to the village

Children from Gretna Primary School tried spying on weddings, clambering up the cherry tree beside the Register Office, and peering through the window. They were checking up to see what stage the weddings had reached, in the hope that there would be a 'scramble' as the party came out. This is an old Scottish custom in which a handful of money was thrown to waiting children by the groom and best man. It seems that some Americans threw out fifty pence pieces, so word quickly got around that waiting for wedding couples could be a lucrative pastime.

With some reluctance, for scrambles were so traditional, Pat Bryden had to put a ban on them. 'It was very distracting to have children's faces appearing at the window whilst the couples were making their solemn vows,' she said. So she asked the brides and grooms not to throw money, and added that it might also prevent the young tree from being damaged.

of Blackshields, near Dalkeith, where they were married by an Episcopalian clergyman.

Mr Surtees refused to forgive his daughter. John Scott was struggling to finish his training for a career in law so the couple had to live very frugally on the little he could earn by working as a private tutor.

'I have married rashly,' John wrote to a friend. 'And have neither house or home to provide for the woman I love.'

He rose early in the morning and worked late into the night, keeping himself awake by wrapping a wet towel around his head. It was five years after their runaway marriage before he was called to the Bar at last. But then he wrote, 'Bessy and I thought all our troubles were over, business was to pour in, and we were to be rich immediately.'

Alas for their hopes. In the first eleven months of that year he received one shilling and in the last month half a guinea. By that time, however, both fathers had become reconciled to the match and settled annuities on them. Then success began to dawn on John and with it he became more and more ambitious. He entered politics and climbed steadily up the ladder, until, as Baron Eldon, he rose to be Lord Chancellor.

In Parliament John was the archetypal reactionary, fighting every reform and improving measure. And despite the fact that he also amassed a fortune of over half a million pounds, the parsimonious habits which he and his wife had been forced into in the early years of their marriage remained with them; Bessy ended life as a recluse.

The second Lord Chancellor to marry north of the border was Lord Erskine, in 1816 – and it was one of the most extraordinary episodes in the whole history of Gretna. The Hon Thomas Erskine was the third son of the Earl of Buchan, he served in both the army and the navy, was called to the English Bar and became a distinguished advocate. His first marriage, to Frances Moore, was unremarkable. She was the daughter of a Member of Parliament and she presented him with a large family of four sons and four daughters before she died in 1805. Thomas was then in his mid-fifties and in that same year he was created Baron Erskine of Restormel Castle and also became Lord Chancellor.

After he had been a widower for some years, he became enamoured of a Miss Sarah Buck, of York Buildings, London. Soon she became his mistress and he had at least two children by her. But when he announced that he intended to marry her there was an outcry from his legitimate offspring. They had no wish to acquire a lowly step-family with whom they might have to share any inheritance. It was for this reason that Thomas decided to elope with his Sarah. He was sixty-six years old. His wit was proverbial – but perhaps he overdid it slightly when he travelled north dressed as an old lady in a 'large leghorn bonnet and long veil'. The landlady of the King's Head Inn in Springfield described him as wearing also 'a long skirted cloak gathered around his neck by a collar. It served well to cover his whole person and he did not take it off when he came into the house.'

At first he was thought to be Sarah Buck's mother and at their request the 'priest' was sent for. Lord Erskine began to question him about the marriage ceremony and it was not long before his disguise was penetrated. Then, according to the landlady, 'Lord Erskine threw off his dress and was married in his own clothes'. Sarah Buck wrapped her children under her cloak during the ceremony to comply with an old belief that illegitimate children would be legitimised by the subsequent marriage of their parents if, during the wedding, they were held 'under the apron strings of their mother'. In any event this was unnecessary, for under Scottish law at that time, a subsequent marriage was held to legitimise children born out of wedlock. The marriage ceremony itself was performed in the downstairs parlour of the King's Head Inn. Such was the rivalry between the 'priests' that one Robert Elliot claimed to have performed this marriage although it was actually David Lang who officiated. He had proof because for some reason Lord Erskine had made him a present of the buttons from his sleeve. The 'priest' was proud to show off this trophy for many years afterwards.

Just as the newlyweds were about to leave, Lord Erskine's eldest son, the Hon Thomas Erskine, drove up. He was as furious as if he had been an enraged parent but was too late to interfere. The encounter was far from friendly, and it was said that Sarah Buck reacted like a virago and disgusted the villagers – who nevertheless gathered round to watch and listen.

Poor Sarah got very little out of her marriage. In 1825 Lord Erskine was travelling by sea to visit his brother in Scotland, when he was afflicted by an inflammation of the chest. He had to be put ashore at Scarborough and he died soon afterwards, leaving Sarah with several children and in very straightened circumstances.

The last of the three Chancellors to be married in Scotland was Henry Peter, later Lord Brougham. He was a Scot, born in Edinburgh, and his long life spanned the four reigns of George III, George IV, William IV and Victoria. He was an advocate of the emancipation of slaves and for better education for the poor in England. It was he who, as advocate for the prosecution, pleaded strongly for a sentence of penal servitude to be passed upon Edward Gibbon Wakefield for his abduction of Ellen Turner (of whom more later). Brougham also has a one-horse carriage named after him.

There appears to be no pressing reason why he should have chosen to marry clandestinely but in the spring of 1819, he went to Coldstream for his wedding to a Mrs Spalding, a widow and niece of Lord Auckland. She had two children and in a letter from Sydney Smith to Lady Grey on 4 January 1819, was said to be 'a showy, long, well-dressed, red and white widow'. Unfortunately she was also something of a hypochondriac, and after the birth of a child two years later, she became a semi-invalid, and thus she was no help to him in his political career. Perhaps it was this sad fact which made him determined to enforce the bill which he eventually steered through parliament and which introduced a residential qualification for marriages in Scotland. This was the 'three week cooling off period' and it was designed to curb the growing number of elopements.

---

The Register Office at Gretna could hardly be plainer or smaller. It is shared by the dentist, and the sound of his drill is not the happiest of wedding music. You might think it was originally designed as a deterrent, but if so it plainly has not been successful. There is talk of building a new one, bigger and better, in keeping with Gretna's new role as a Gateway to Scotland. One and a half million visitors a year are expected to call at the proposed new Centre, sponsored by the Scottish Tourist Board, the Development Agency, and the local councils.

CHAPTER FIVE

# The Marrying-trade and its 'Priests'

The old road from Carlisle to Glasgow passed through Longtown in Cumberland where it crossed the River Esk and continued on over an area of rough scrubland, known as the Solway Moss, towards Scotland. The border was, and still is, defined by another small river, the Sark, which winds and eddies between sandy brown banks, and flows beneath the single arch of an old humpbacked bridge and the road. Less than a mile away lies Gretna Green. It is a small village even now, but in the eighteenth century it was no more than a cluster of little white-washed cottages, a church and one or two farms. The building, now known as the Old Blacksmith's Shop was built sometime between 1705 and 1713. Nowadays the road leads first into Springfield, but this village only came into existence in 1791 when Sir William Maxwell, Baronet of Springkell, sold off one of his farms in small lots for building. Springfield adjoins Gretna Green so closely that it is difficult for an outsider to know where one starts and the other finishes. Both were involved in the marrying business, so that many a 'Gretna marriage' actually took place in Springfield.

Back in the days when the road through Longtown was the most direct route, it was inevitable that the two inns in Springfield, being the first hostelries over the border, should claim a great deal of the marriage-trade. They were the Maxwell Arms and the Queen's Head, the latter sometimes called indeed The Marriage House.

Peter Orlando Hutchinson, who visited the area in the early 1840s and wrote a book called *Chronicles of Gretna Green*, said of the Queen's Head, 'This hostelrie is a glorious ruin. It forms a coin or angle of two streets, it is entered from the principal one by a door in the centre of the façade, there is a sash window on either side and three above. The splendour of the interior has faded, on the left hand on entering there is a kitchen, on the right hand a parlour. Visitors to this shrine have

In the old marriage room of the Sark Bridge Tollbar, about a dozen visitor's books are on show. There are over a million signatures from the past decade alone – and other older books are upstairs for safe keeping. Almost every entry tells a snippet of a story.

8.7.85 – Conny and Rene Huppi, from Zürich, Switzerland – 'Our grandparents married in 1912 in this place.'

30.7.84 – Judith and Adrian, from Hanworth, Birmingham – Married in Gretna at 3 pm today. Will call again.

31.7.84 – Terry and Jennifer from Stoke on Trent – He asked me to marry him again.

1.8.84 – Dee Hulley from Overport, Durban. 'I have not yet snared him.'

2.8.84 – M Cunlim and S James. Pontypridd, S Wales – Getting married in about 2 hours and 25 minutes at Annan – (Gretna full up!)

3.8.84 – Ron and Ruby Jones, Weston-super-mare, Avon – Too late, knot's already tied.

3.8.84 – R Turner, Leek, Staffs – Came here to refresh my life.

Same date – S Harrison, NSW Australia – Came here to help above with her project.

9.8.84 – Eileen and Colin Kerr from Wattle Vale, Brisbane, NSW Australia – Here at long last.

14.8.84 – Christine Marnoch from Fife – Fiancé disappeared back to car, fast!

17.8.84 – Christine Owen from London – If only I had a man to marry.

18.8.84 – Fiona and Archie, Glasgow – Mr & Mrs A Baillie were married here (my aunt and uncle)

25.8.84 – Ramona Davidson, from Queensland Australia – I knew if I stuck to him long enough I'd one day see Bonnie Scotland.

liberally amused themselves with writing with diamond rings, their names or those of their friends, mottoes and amatory verse on the panes of the windows'. One of these had 'Lord Erskine' scratched twice over, though it is most unlikely that it was his own handiwork. On the window of the bedroom above the parlour someone had written:

> Transporting hope to clasp the charming Miss,
> In her fair arms, to what unequalled bliss;
> What joys I tasted, when, from Gretna's shrine,
> I drew the maid, and swore she should be mine – AH

At the end of the eighteenth century a new bridge was built over the River Sark. This was close to the present bridge over which traffic speeds between Carlisle and Glasgow, bypassing Gretna. The old turnpike took travellers directly into the village, avoiding Springfield. A toll house was erected on the Scottish side of the border to collect dues from the travellers – and what an ideal situation this commanded for getting in on the runaway marriages! The landlord there soon took up the trade, as well as toll collecting and the sale of 'ale, porter and spirituous liquors'. The establishment of the turnpike and the beginning of regular coaching runs from Carlisle to Glasgow made it necessary for Gretna to have an inn of quality, not only to cater for travellers but also to provide relays of horses. For this purpose Gretna Hall was converted into an hotel; it had previously been a family mansion built by the owner of the estate in 1710. Gretna Hall Hotel played an important role in romantic elopements and took the cream of the trade.

There were one or two other inns or beer shops in Gretna. All these establishments competed with each other for custom and marriages also took place in private houses or even out of doors. Both Gretna Green and Springfield were so well prepared that a couple could arrive at any time of the day or night and get married within five minutes, 'even though no forerunner had been sent ahead to prepare for their coming'. But, often the business arrangements for the marriages were negotiated when the runaways stopped in Carlisle; there the horses were changed for the last time prior to the final dash over the border. The postillions who took over the final drive had contacts with one or other of the Gretna marriage houses and of course, that was where they carried the eloping couples, no matter what orders they were given. Plenty of people were willing to officiate but in effect the trade was cornered by a few self-styled 'priests'. They made a good living out of it and there were some extraordinary characters among them.

George Gordon was an old soldier who dressed for his part in an enormous cocked hat, red coat, jackboots and carried a heavy old sword.

When someone asked him by what authority he officiated at marriages he would reply, 'I have a special licence from the Government and I pay fifty pounds a year for it.' This was a downright lie but there were many who believed him.

One of the best known of the 'priests' was a big, rough, hard-drinking Borderer named Joseph Pasley. He was born in about 1730, the son of a dissenting clergyman, in a small village just south of the border, a mile or so from Gretna. In his early teens he became bound apprentice to a tobacconist but he soon left for a more adventurous life and became a fisherman, working with a notorious character known as 'Auld Watty Coulthard'. Watty was a smuggler as well as a fisherman and was himself one of the first of the 'priests'. He lived in a smokey hovel, close to the Solway, with a scolding wife, from both of which he was glad to escape. He usually performed his marriage ceremonies out of doors among the whins beside the beach.

Joseph Pasley as a young man was handsome, tall, and well-built. He was reputed to be so strong he could bend a poker over his bare arm and straighten a horseshoe with his mighty hands. He may sound like the brawny blacksmith legend portrays as the typical 'priest' but that was never his occupation. He made an excellent 'mate' for Watty, for he was not only strong but a fearless fisherman and smuggler and since he had been given an elementary education, he was able to act as clerk at the weddings. Then came a day when Auld Watty went to the Isle of Man to collect some contraband brandy and left his assistant to perform a marriage on his own. Joseph Pasley, then in his mid-twenties, was quick to realise that he could tie the knot just as well as his master. Moreover, he could not help noticing that the job provided an easy source of income and very soon he managed to set up in the marriage business for himself.

For some time he worried as to whether this trade was strictly legal; not that he had any real qualms about performing the ceremonies any more than he had about smuggling or salmon poaching. It was simply that at the back of his mind there was some furtive link between the two occupations, so he moved around secretly by back lanes and field paths to get to the houses where he was called to officiate. When he wrote out the marriage certificate it was not only badly written and misspelt, but almost illegible and signed with a false name such as 'John Brown', as an added precaution.

It came as a great shock to him when, a few years after he had taken up this new trade, he was summoned to London for an important trial in which the evidence hinged on one of his marriages. Scared as to what might happen to him, Joseph Pasley decided to consult an eminent Scottish barrister who was able to explain to him the legal requirements of an irregular marriage. He was told that to use a false name was certainly unlawful and he was advised that, if possible, he should destroy the original certificate and substitute another signed with his own name. This new certificate was to state that he was merely a witness to the declaration of the parties that they considered themselves to be married. In effect he had committed no misdemeanour whatsoever. What an uplift it must have given him to know that such a lucrative and expanding occupation was absolutely legal! After that, with a full understanding of the requirements of a marriage under Scottish law, Joseph was able to walk openly to the weddings. He dressed smartly for the occasion and began to grow in stature, both literally and figuratively.

For the last forty years of his life, Joseph Pasley drank one Scots pint of brandy every day (equal to two and a quarter pints in England) and in those days it was said to be stronger too! On one occasion he and a drinking friend, one Ned Turner, sat down to an anker of cognac – a barrel containing ten gallons. In two and a half days they had drunk it dry and were so furious that it had run out so soon that they kicked the empty cask to pieces. On another occasion, towards the end of his 'priesthood', two couples arrived at the same time, both in desperate haste to be married. He performed the ceremonies together and afterwards it was discovered that he had made a mistake and married the wrong brides and bridegrooms! He shrugged off the error as a 'trifling mistake' and simply advised the couples to 'juist sort yersel's oot'. He often remarked that though he was paid well for marrying folk, he could make his fortune in a week if he could divorce them as quickly.

Over the years he degenerated into an enormous, coarse old man, weighing about twenty-five stones and he was over eighty when he died in 1814. His reputation was such that there is one story of how when he lay dying, several carriages and four drove into the village at speed, making such a noise and clatter that Joseph Pasley opened his eyes at the sound. They contained three loving couples who had driven like fury over the Solway Moss. With great effort he summoned his strength and sent someone down to fetch up these clients and declared his willingness to wed them. This he did, even as he lay there, and it was further said that when the business was over he found himself no less than £300 the richer.

Another 'priest' of that time was David Lang, who was in fact the nephew of Joseph Pasley. Lang was born in 1755 and in his youth he became a pedlar, walking from place to place carrying a pack containing small items of drapery and haberdashery which he sold to housewives and their daughters in villages and on lonely farms. He worked his way southwards into Lancashire and there one day a press-gang caught him. These legalised kidnappers carried David Lang off, as they had many a young and able-bodied man, and forced him to serve in the British Navy.

David Lang spent several years at sea, until eventually his ship was captured by John Paul Jones, considered by the English to be a pirate but by the Americans as the father of their navy. Jones was a borderer famed for his seafaring exploits against the British during the American War of Independence. Probably David Lang had little cause to love either master and one dark night, when the ship was close to the Solway shore, he escaped and made his way home. Before long he set himself up in business as a 'priest'. He was then about thirty-eight, a fine-looking man with a large full face, an amiable expression and dark intelligent eyes. He dressed in a broad-brimmed hat and dark suit with a white stock, a clerical outfit in accordance with his self-important air, earning him the nickname of 'Bishop Lang'.

A few years before Joseph Pasley died his granddaughter, Anne Graham, the 'belle of the village' married Robert Elliot, who was the son of a Northumberland farmer and worked with a stagecoach company. This wedding took place in the village church, as was considered proper because very few local people ever married in the irregular way. From then on Robert Elliot helped his grandfather-in-law with the marriage trade.

About thirty years later Elliot had a book published titled *Memoires of Gretna Green*, which he dictated to a clergyman called the Reverend Caleb Browne. To publicise this work he sent a document which he called a 'cercler' to various newspapers saying this book contained 'an accurate account of remarkable elopements, pursuits, anecdotes etc never before published'. He claimed that in twenty-eight years he had married 7,744 persons but it is likely that some of the elopements he wrote about occurred before he took up the trade. Robert and Ann Elliot had a handicapped daughter, who was deaf and dumb, and one night this poor girl set fire to the box bed in which she slept. The old marriage registers were stored on the canopy above the bed and unfortunately they were all destroyed. Even if Elliot's figures were exaggerated, it must be remembered that other 'priests' were operating in Gretna at the same time and that irregular marriages were also being performed at Coldstream, Lamberton, Edinburgh and in other towns and villages along the Scottish side of the border.

At about this same time, in the 1830s, the Sark Tollbar was run by a Simon Beattie, 'a large, stalwart man, taller than many and fatter than most'. He spoke a rough mixture of Cumberland and Scottish dialects which was difficult for a southerner to comprehend. He had, however, a very keen eye for business. 'Not a being was said to pass over the bridge but Simon scanned him searchingly with his eye,' wrote Hutchinson. 'First through the little diagonal window such as all tollhouses possess and then from his front door, and if there was anything in the stranger's appearance that looked as if he might be seeking wedlock, Simon would courteously but bluntly enter into conversation with him.

'Rumour had it that he once waylaid an old woman and her nephew as they were returning from Carlisle market and almost married them regardless of their protestations. On another occasion a man travelling the road, a stranger to those parts, chanced to meet a woman of whom he enquired the way. Simon pounced upon them as they conversed and entreated them forthwith to swear hymnal faith and love to each other till death them should part.' It was some time before they could persuade him that they were strangers, and had never met before. But even then Simon saw no reason why he should not wed them!

The great hiring fairs in Carlisle at Martinmas and Whitsuntide produced big business for Gretna. The lads and lassies would set out on foot and in wagons and carts to be wed there because it was cheaper than church and there were no banns to be put up. Deploring this, a newspaper report on the events at Martinmas in 1842 recorded that 'between 4 o'clock on Saturday morning and Sunday evening last, not less than 45 couples were married by Mr Simon Beattie of the Sark Tollbar, besides all the business done in the same way by the worthy "bishop" Mr John Linton of Gretna Hall'.

Simon Beattie had the advantage of numbers, but John Linton had the most profitable part of the trade. He became the landlord of Gretna Hall Hotel in 1825 and it was he who really built up its reputation as a marriage house. He had previously been a 'gentleman's gentleman' as valet to Sir James Graham of Netherby Hall, near Carlisle. Netherby deserves a passing mention for its romantic association with the poem by Sir Walter Scott, which told of 'Young Lochinvar' who came out of the west to rescue fair Ellen, who was being forced into marriage with 'a laggard in love and a dastard in war'. But, 'ere he alighted at Netherby Gate/The bride had consented, the gallant came late'. Notwithstanding this, Lochinvar swept his lady from her nuptials and carried her off on his fiery steed.

John Linton was a man of some refinement and dignity and when he took over Gretna Hall he fitted it out as a first class hotel and posting house. It was described as the principal aristocratic and fashionable resort of runaways, a comely looking establishment with fine grounds, where one could get a fair relay of horses and 'peradventure good entertainment'. Hutchinson found the place 'altogether tastefully laid out' and was impressed that several stacks of chimneys rose 'exhiliratingly' over the whole building. He set great store by chimneys, asserting that an abundance of them betokened comfort and warmth. In front of the hotel was a lawn, green and pleasing, garnished with trees and evergreens and a carriage drive of 200 yards. Adjoining this were shady and labyrinthine walks where lovers could saunter at will in the cool of the evening.

With an astute eye to the marriage-trade, John Linton set apart a special parlour for these ceremonies. Since his clients were the richest of the visitors to Gretna, they were also the most likely to be pursued, and on many occasions there would be a furious knocking at the door even before the 'priest' had spoken the necessary words to unite the couple. They would be refused entry until the ceremony was completed, then Linton would hustle the newlyweds through his private apartment and into a secret chamber. There they could hide while he suavely but firmly dealt with the pursuing party by informing the angry relatives that they were too late, that the young couple had been married and had left.

At first David Lang, his son, Simon or some other 'priest', was called in to officiate at the Gretna Hall weddings; John Linton merely acted as one of the witnesses. He soon learned the tricks of the trade however, and within a couple of years took over the office of 'priest' himself. Later on his son, Richard, became his partner and in this way and by always making sure that one or other was at home, they were able to provide a twenty-four hour service.

Simon Lang took over after the death of his father David, the pedlar, in 1827 and he became the only 'priest' of importance who was actually born in the village. Simon was a weaver by trade, and lived in Springfield in a 'single-end' as the Scots called a cottage of only one room. Hutchinson wrote of that one room that it 'embraced at once all the varied attributes of parlour, kitchen, bedroom, nursery and larder. The floor was neither boards nor flagstones, nor brick, nor tiles nor lime-ash, it was nothing but plain unsophisticated mother earth, beaten flat – or rather not flat for it was all ups and downs.

47

'The tables and chairs were made of native-grown ash, pine or oak and no two resembled each other in pattern. Some pieces of peat were piled on the dusty hearth and the flickering flame licked the bottom of a smokey pot. The lime-washed walls once white, were brown by age and neglect, a few popular prints and one or two popular ballads were stuck upon the walls by means of wafers (gummed papers) at the corners. Mrs Lang's appearance and vesture suited, not unmeetly the poverty around.' Simon looked much more like a weaver than a 'priest' but he had a good reputation and a fair name for integrity; it was said of him, 'His is a kind of happy medium in stature, neither tall nor short, in face somewhat spare, and not much otherwise in limb.' Though he had a grave countenance Simon Lang was said to have a keen sense of humour. Living almost opposite to him was another 'priest' known as 'Tam the Piper'. The two men would stand at their doors and if Simon saw a couple looking as if they were about to approach Tam, he would call out 'Don't ye heed that big man there, he's juist out of the asylum last week – you'll be wrong if ye go near him.' Tam was well able to reply in kind and the good-natured rivalry often provided amusement in the street.

Tam the Piper's real name was Thomas Little. He was a man cast in the same mould as Joseph Pasley, weighing twenty-three stones and always ready for a drink. He loved a joke and earned his nickname by playing the bagpipes when trade was slack. In front of his house he hung a painted sign with the words 'The Gretna Wedding Inn'. The picture portrayed a bridegroom, a fierce-looking officer in a scarlet tunic covered in embroidery and gold lace, a lady holding hands with him, her eyes downcast modestly beneath a large feathered hat and a blacksmith kneeling on the opposite side of the anvil with his assistant alongside, both of them grinning merrily. True to tradition the background was of a blacksmith's shop and it was probably painted by a local artist. The setting owed more to popular fiction than to reality.

Tam showed considerable initiative in promoting the marriage trade. Because some customers always came from the area of Brampton in Cumberland, he made an arrangement with the proprietor of the Howard Arms in that town to send any amorous couples to him. Those who came to Tam were much more likely to travel in a tub-gig, a type of governess cart often used by families in the borders, rather than by post-chaise. He was also a regular attendant at Langholm Fair, to which he carried his sign from The Gretna Wedding Inn, setting it up outside a tent. Robert Hyslop, in *Echoes from the Border Hills*, describes one of Tam's weddings at the Handfasting Fair. 'Imagine the place crowded with half drunken men. A young woman pushes her way to the front, half dragging a hesitating swain. She is not, on this her wedding day, carrying a bouquet of fragrant flowers or white heather, but as she elbows her way to Tam she is eating a thick slice of gingerbread, which perhaps, though it is not exactly elegant is not to be wondered at, considering her early breakfast and long tramp to the fair.

'Tam puts the usual questions and these being answered, just about as coherently as if the man had been sober, he declares them married persons and gives the bride her "lines" which, probably with an eye to the future, she is eager to have and which she deposits in her bodice along with what remains of the gingerbread.'

Tam was illiterate so his wife wrote out the certificate while he went through the ceremony. No registers seem to have been kept by him but undoubtedly he was a well-known character among the 'priests' of the mid-nineteenth century.

Though most of those who acted as 'priests' boasted of making vast sums from their calling, the money seems to have been dissipated away as quickly as it came. Simon Beattie appears to have been the only one to have possessed the Scots virtue of thrift; he saved enough to enable him to take up the tenancy of a farm in his later years. He died unmarried and left his registers to his sister. Unfortunately, she was nervous about the legality of holding them and when she found herself pestered by enquirers she became so worried that she burned them all.

When Simon Beattie left the Tollbar it was eagerly taken over by John Murray. Murray's mother was a cousin of Thomas Telford, the great road builder, and as a young man John worked for him as a stonemason. It was not until he moved to Annan in connection with his work that he realised that marrying could be a more lucrative business than masonry; it was with this in mind that he negotiated the takeover of the lease of the Tollbar in 1843. John Murray soon gained a reputation for the large number of persons that he married and also for his very low charges. He seems to have relied on increasing his turnover and did the weddings at bargain prices. His usual fee was 7s 6d (37½p) with an additional 1s 6d (7½p) for each of the two witnesses, making a total of half a guinea (55p). On occasions he was known to have charged as little as sixpence (2½p). His ceremony was abbreviated to its barest essentials.

'Are you both unmarried persons?'

'Yes.'

'Have you got a ring?' If neither of the parties had a ring Murray supplied them with one that looked rather like a curtain ring; this was placed on the bride's finger. It was never truly a necessary part of a marriage but somehow it gave a semblance of tradition.

'Do you take this woman you hold by the right hand to be your lawful wedded wife?'

'Yes.'

'Do you take this man to be your lawful wedded husband?'

'Yes.'

'Before God and these witnesses I declare you married persons and whom God hath joined let no man put asunder.'

Murray's cut-price weddings attracted plenty of customers. He sometimes found it difficult to get witnesses as the Tollbar had no houses nearby. But even as far back as that foreigners occasionally appeared. 'Claverhouse' (the pseudonym of Miss Meloria Smith of Gretna Hall) in her book *Irregular Border Marriages* records: 'One day two Germans wished him to marry them; Murray could not make out if they were both single persons, or indeed understand what they were talking about. He saw approaching a young lady of the neighbourhood and rushed out imploring her to dismount and assist him – but she would have nothing to do with the case. On another occasion Sir John Heron-Maxwell was driving from Carlisle but Murray refused to open the tollgates, saying "Na, na, Captain – I'll no let ye through, ye maun come inside." Finding there was no help for it, Sir John went into the Tollbar to find a couple who wished to be married but could not give the fee demanded. Murray wanted Captain Maxwell to be a witness to their promise to send the money. All was arranged and they were married.'

John Murray was a shrewd and intelligent man. His registers were well-kept and in the period from 1843, when he took over the Tollbar, until the Lord Brougham Act in 1856, he listed almost 8,000 marriages.

'There's no need for ye to gang up to the Hall,' he used to tell people. 'I can marry ye juist as well, it'll no cost ye as much and it'll last juist as lang.'

His ambition was to take more of the quality trade from John Linton at the Hall but he had neither accommodation for people, nor stabling for horses, so the best of the custom continued to pass him by. To rectify this he decided to build a hotel himself but unfortunately he sited it on

The Old Blacksmith's Shop, Gretna Green. (*Dumfries and Galloway Regional Library Service*)

Fun at a mock wedding! The Gretna Hall Blacksmith's Shop. (Spot the naughty lady with the camera *see page 8*.)

Sarah Anne Child, painted as the Countess of Westmorland by George Romney in 1785. (*The Earl of Jersey*)

John Fane, Earl of Westmorland in about 1785 by George Romney. (*The Earl of Jersey*)

'A Fleet Wedding. Between a brisk young Sailor & his Landlady's Daughter at Rederiff.' 1747. (*Reproduced by kind permission of the trustees of the British Museum*)

Miss Pat Bryden MBE officiating at a marriage at Gretna Register Office.

Gretna Hall. (*Dumfries and Galloway Regional Library Service*)

Joseph Paisley the celebrated Gretna-Green Parson'. (*Mary Evans Picture Library*)

David Lang

'Fillial Affection or A Trip to Gretna Green' by Rowlandson, 1785. (*Reproduced by kind permission of th*
*trustees of the British Museum*)

Henry Peter, 1st Lord Brougham by Thomas Lawrence. (*National Portrait Gallery*)

John Peel

Ken Dodd at the 'marriage' of Neville King and Joan Lambert. Jim Jackson officiates.

An early photograph of the Sark Tollbar.

Kitty Barnes by J. Holmes. (*In a privat
collection*)

Thomas, Lord Cochrane by P. H. Stroehling. (*In a private Scottish collection*)

the English side of the Sark. This was not as foolish as it sounds for he expected that couples would stay there, simply cross the bridge for their wedding at the Tollbar in Scotland and then return to spend part of their honeymoon, or at least some of their money and also stable their horses, at his hotel. Alas it never worked out that way, for Lord Brougham's Marriage Act came into effect the year the building was completed. For many years the hotel was used as a private residence, but it has now been reconverted to its original use and is known as the Gretna Chase Hotel.

Fees for the marriages were elastic but the 'priest' asked as much as he thought the bridegroom could afford; he became adept at assessing his clients by their dress and bearing, coupled with information from the postillion who had brought them from Carlisle on the last stage of their journey. Five to twenty pounds were fairly normal payments but there are records of extreme amounts in either direction. The Earl of Westmorland and Lord Deerhurst apparently each paid a hundred guineas for their weddings and also on the high side was the sum of £60 paid by the elderly Lord Erskine for his marriage to Sarah Buck. One generous and happy bridegroom paid the postboys with a wineglass filled with golden guineas and gave a tumblerful to the coachman. On the other hand farm labourers from either side of the border could expect to be married for about three shillings (15p) and a dram of whisky.

There is an authenticated story about one marriage performed for only 2½d (little more than one penny). This was for a couple of paupers who had run away from the workhouse; the bridegroom was a widower with four children and the bride, who had been his childhood sweetheart, was a widow and had three children of her own. On another occasion, a tramp was married to a 'buxom female pedlar' and they bargained with the 'priest' and finally paid with a lady's side comb, worth 1½d, a pocket handkerchief which was worth 6d, and 2½d in cash, making a total in cash and kind of 10d (about 4½p). While the hotel charges of a wedding at Gretna Hall on 15 August 1825 were:

| | | |
|---|---:|---:|
| Wine and Brandy | 3s | 2d |
| Breakfast | 4 | 6 |
| Postboys eating | 5 | 0 |
| Horse's Hay | 2 | 0 |
| Witness | £2 2 | 0 |
| Wedding Room | 10 | 6 |
| total | £3 7 | 2 |

The 'priest' John Linton would have claimed his fee in addition.

One elderly lady, writing in 1897, gave this graphic account of her

The bakers are eager to make a wedding cake for that special day, and flowers, buttonholes and bouquets can be easily arranged. The photographers will not only take pictures at the Register Office, at the blacksmith's shops, and in the specially designed garden of an hotel, they will make a video of it, too. The taxi service with beautifully dressed wedding cars is always available – or lovers can be really romantic and hire a horse and carriage.

marriage at Gretna, which had taken place sixty years previously. She had been assisted by her mother-in-law-to-be who had 'sent a note saying that a carpet bag was gone down to the hotel ready with all I might require for present use and that they knew all the arrangements about horses and orders for relays as far as in those days they could be ordered.

'At 8 o'clock in the evening we started. My wedding ring had to be purchased and sandwiches and wine replenished while the horses were being changed. Returning to the hotel we were off again after getting a Bank Post Bill changed for £320. On we went all night, all day on Sunday and Sunday night, arriving at Carlisle so early that the ostlers and landlord had to be called up.

'The post-boys took us where they knew the nearest spot on Scotch soil, which was a wayside cottage. At four o'clock in the morning, April 29th, dripping wet, an old woman in a nightcap put her head out and in a few minutes came down and let us into a small carpetless room, containing a few chairs and a shabby desk. Presently an oldish man came in and in broad Scotch said – "I suppose you've come to be married. We charge pretty high on these occasions."

' "What?"

' "£30."

'It had to be given, no time to question and two guineas for postboys as witnesses. £1 for the room where the marriage was held and 5s for postboys' beer. Marriage Certificate given. Then the postboys said they would take us to a nice hotel at a place called Longtown and there we arrived, more dead than alive with nervous tension, but had not been pursued.'

In the early days of irregular marriages consummation was regarded as the best evidence of union and for this reason marriages were often performed in inns where a bedroom was always kept ready for immediate use. In *A Tour of Scotland* by Pennant, published in 1780, it states 'If pursuit of friends proves very hot; and there is not time for the ceremony, the frightened pair are advised to slip into bed; are shewn to the pursuers, who imagining that they are irrecoverably united, retire and leave them to consummate their unfinished loves.' On one occasion there was not even time for the gentleman to remove his boots. The reason for this lies in the ancient laws regarding spousals which, prior to Lord Hardwicke's Marriage Act, could take two forms. One was the contract *per verba de futuro* which was little more than an engagement, a promise to marry in the future. If this declaration was not followed by consummation it could be broken later by mutual consent but if the union was consummated then the contract was binding for life.

The second form of contract was *per verba de præsenti*. In this form the pair made vows before witnesses using such phrases as 'I do take thee to my wife' and 'I do take thee to my husband'. This was an irrevocable commitment which could never be broken and this was certainly the form used by all the 'priests' in Scotland. Not surprisingly the difference between the two forms was difficult for the ordinary person to understand and it was to make sure that all requirements were satisfied that the bedroom was always kept ready. At Sark Tollbar this custom was pared to a farcical limit but still felt to be essential. A special bedroom was set apart and as soon as the marriage had been performed, the wife of the 'priest' would conduct the newly married couple into it. They were told to lie on the bed, a coverlet was thrown over them and the door closed. Within seconds the door was opened again and the lovers told they could go. They had had time for only a brief kiss but since the 'priest' could argue that they had been to bed together, he felt that the contract was properly sealed.

'Claverhouse' writes: 'The inn at which Elliot married the folk was kept by a Mrs Johnstone who, together with a servant called Sawney, was a true friend to distressed couples. Mrs Johnstone and Sawney, in co-operation and alone, must have soothed many a stormy scene, got many young people out of difficulties and probably prevented more bloodshed than is generally supposed.' However, in at least one instance they were unsuccessful and murder followed an elopement. The story is taken from Elliot's *Memoires*.

A young English lady, the daughter of a wealthy old baronet from the Midlands, had fixed her affections on the son of a neighbouring gentleman of considerable landed property, who had paid his addresses to her for some time. Both families appeared to approve of their courtship, until it became known that the young gentleman's father was in very 'embarrassed circumstances' owing to his fondness for gambling. Most of the family estate had to be sold and the son, now relatively poor, was forbidden to visit the house of his lady-love. At the same time, her father gave her to understand that she must think no more of her lover, but prepare to receive one of his choosing, who he had already invited to court his daughter. Nevertheless she managed to keep up a correspondence with her true lover and he persuaded her to elope with him to Gretna. They set off on the very night that her new suitor was to arrive to ask for her hand.

The baronet, frantic with rage on discovering that his daughter had gone, armed himself with pistols and set off in pursuit. The new suitor accompanied him and they both swore to kill the young man should they overtake the couple. Meanwhile, the young pair arrived at Gretna and lost no time in summoning Mr Pasley, who afterwards declared they were the handsomest and best matched couple he had ever married. Upon completion of the ceremony the young gentleman took Mr Pasley aside and briefly told him the circumstances and that he expected pursuit, and asked what he would recommend them to do. The usual course was adopted. The timid, blushing young lady was conducted to the nuptial chamber in order that the consummation of their marriage might be added as a seal of their union.

In the middle of the night the inmates of the inn were alarmed by the sudden arrival of a chaise and four horses, driven at top speed. The bride's father and his companion alighted and began to thunder at the door and window shutters with the butts of their pistols. The frightened landlord opened the door only just in time to prevent it being broken down. Fiercely the father interrogated the landlord, threatening him with instant death if he did not show him where the fugitives were hidden. The landlord took him upstairs as slowly as his impatient and unwelcome guest would permit, endeavouring to soothe the old man with the usual commonplace consolations for his arrival which had come too late. Finally he mentioned that since the marriage had already been consummated, there was nothing he could do but 'grin and bear it'. The old gentleman reached the landing and was close to the door of the room in which his daughter and her husband were sleeping. He instantly rushed against it and it yielded to his force, so that he burst into the room and stood before his terrified daughter, pointing his pistol at her husband. The young bride jumped from the bed to come between them – but alas! She was too late. Her father fired his fatal shot and she collapsed unconscious upon her husband's lifeless body, the blood flowing from the wound in his breast and staining her nightdress. The beautiful young bride was now a widow.

One servant, bolder than the rest, would have seized the father but was deterred by the weapon he still held and with which he threatened to shoot the first person who should attempt to thwart him. With the assistance of his friend he raised his daughter from the floor and hastily wrapping her in some cloaks, carried her off in his chaise. They drove off immediately before she had recovered her senses.

At the trial that followed, the counsel for the old man made it appear that he had shot only in self-defence and to the best of Elliot's belief, he got off scot free, but found reason to repent of his cruelty, for his daughter never recovered from the shock. She died soon afterwards, broken-hearted. After this, finding himself hated and shunned by all his former friends and neighbours, he retired to the Continent where he spent the rest of his life.

# CHAPTER SIX

# Kitty Barnes and Thomas, Lord Cochrane

When Thomas, Lord Cochrane, heir to the Earl of Dundonald, married Miss Kitty Barnes, he did so in the most simple manner of Scottish tradition. The extraordinary account of their courtship and marriage has been preserved in his own book *Autobiography of a Seaman* and in an affidavit signed by him shortly before he died in 1860. But, most moving of all, it is recorded in a verbatim report based on an interview given by Kitty, Countess of Dundonald, before the House of Lords on 24 July 1862. The language may appear stilted, the facts almost incredible, but the words of this elderly widow ring with truth and pride as they bring alive that far away time when Thomas swept her off to Scotland to be married. In his autobiography he wrote 'without a particle of romance in my composition, my life has been one of the most romantic on record'.

It was in the year 1812 that Lord Cochrane first saw Kitty as she walked in a school crocodile in Hyde Park, London. He had just returned from sea, where he had been one of the heroes of England's fight against Napoleon. Kitty was an orphan and lived with her aunt and uncle, John Simpson, in their comfortable house in Portland Place. From her mother, who had been a Spanish dancer, she had inherited an ivory complexion and glossy hair, so dark it was almost black, which she wore in ringlets. She had a slim supple figure and a naturally graceful carriage. In temperament she took after her father, an Englishman, being of a calm and gentle disposition but with hidden reserves of strength that would stand her in good stead in the turbulent, adventurous years to come.

A few days after he had noticed Kitty walking in the school crocodile, Thomas Cochrane contrived to meet John Simpson and was invited to the house and formally introduced to Kitty. He made no attempt to hide his interest in her, and her uncle and aunt were suitably impressed by this bold, dashing man, aware that he was not only a naval hero but also heir to the Earl of Dundonald. He was at that time living with his rich uncle, Basil Cochrane.

Thomas was thirty-seven years old at that time while Kitty was only sixteen but to her he never seemed old. He was tall and handsome, with curly, sandy-coloured hair, and when he told her of his exploits at sea, they sounded just as exciting to her as those of Raleigh or Drake. While he was in his mid-twenties he had been put in command of a sloop called *Speedy* and with immense courage and daring, he had captured fifty enemy ships, 122 guns and 543 men, after which Nelson gave him the nickname 'Wolf of the Sea'. He has been described by his biographer Ian Grimble, as 'next only to Nelson, the most brilliant and daring naval commander Britain has ever known'. On one occasion he sailed into Plymouth sound with tall golden candlesticks fixed to each masthead, a flamboyant gesture that was greeted by cheers from the crowds who lined the harbour to welcome the ship home. Kitty never doubted him when he failed in his attempt to bring about the destruction of the French fleet. He explained that it had been no fault of his but that the blame rested with his admiral, who had cautiously stayed too far out at sea, and had not taken advantage of the opening that he, Thomas Cochrane, had made.

After twenty years at sea, he had returned to England, and had become a member of the House of Commons. 'I want to do something to help our seamen,' he told Kitty. 'The conditions under which they serve are appalling – funds which should go to equip the ships and pay the men are often misappropriated. There are scoundrels who line their pockets at the expense of our gallant sailors!'

Kitty listened; she didn't really understand but she was impressed and flattered, charmed and amused by him. They talked and laughed together and Thomas, as she had now come to call him, made no bones of the fact that he was courting her. In the proper manner, he sought the approval of her guardian and within a few weeks proposed marriage to her. How could she resist such a swash-buckling suitor? With her aunt, Kitty began to think excitedly about preparations for her coming wedding.

Then one day Thomas came to her, rushing into the house, filling it as he always did with the vibrancy of his personality, he grasped her hands in his with an air of great excitement about him.

'Kitty – let us elope together. Get married quietly and quickly, in Scotland.'

She was shocked. 'Oh, no! Why should we do such a thing?'

'Because my uncle is pressing me to marry someone else, and I will not.'

'But Thomas, you are not just a boy! You have been in command of ships and fleets – surely you may marry whom you will?'

There is an old Pictish custom in which the groom takes the bride's name and this was revived in December 1987, when Jill Annandale married Neil Turner. They travelled from Preston to the Register Office at Annan because Jill had long cherished a dream that when she got married it would be in the district whose name she bears.

She has no brothers, and the family name would have died out if Neil had not agreed to adopt it. The bride's father, William Annandale, who accompanied his daughter for the ceremony, was very pleased. Neil Annandale (né Turner) and his bride, whose name was unchanged, revived an ancient precedent.

'Most assuredly I can, and of course, I will. But you know I am only on half-pay. My father is constantly in debt. He cannot help me at all, in fact we both have to rely a great deal on my uncle. I don't wish to fall out with him if it can be avoided.'

'Then perhaps we should wait. Why hurry into marriage if it will anger him?'

'Because I am in love with you, Mouse. I will marry no other.'

Those ardent words and his use of that pet name he often used for her, almost beguiled her into agreement but Kitty was not entirely convinced. 'I – I don't understand why there must be this hurry and secrecy, Thomas.'

'Because I'm so afraid he will find some way to part us. How dare he presume to choose a wife for me!'

'You know I have no fortune – perhaps you would be wise to do as your uncle wishes.' It was hard to say – but if he wished to be free—

'Never! His choice is an insult to me! The fortune that woman has was made from swindling officers and men of the Navy. I have told him I abhor the idea of marrying for money. I cannot and I will not. I will only marry you, Kitty – so let us run away together—'

'You ask too much, Thomas. What would people think of me?'

'I care not what people think.'

'But I do. I have little other than my good reputation. No. I cannot do it.'

'Please, Mouse—'

'No. I will have a proper church wedding – or I will not be married at all.' She remained firm in that resolve, despite his pleading; at last Lord Cochrane saw that she was determined and he left. A few days later his servant, Richard Carter, came to the house with a message that his master was very ill. Would she not relent and agree to marry him as he suggested? Kitty did not know what to do. She talked the matter over with her aunt but still the idea of a runaway, clandestine marriage seemed too shocking to contemplate. Then another member of Thomas's family, Captain Nathaniel Cochrane, called upon them with an even more urgent entreaty.

'Thomas is very, very ill. He may even be dying—'

Kitty gasped, deeply distressed.

'Miss Barnes, he begs that he may see you, but his uncle has given instructions that you are not to be allowed into the house.'

'Then what can I do?'

'Just walk in the Square, so that he may watch you from his window. It means so much to him.'

Quickly she fetched her bonnet and shawl and on the arm of Captain Nathaniel, walked slowly along the street.

'There – do you see him?' She looked up at the house and saw Thomas at the window, supported by his servant. He looked so pale, almost as if he was a corpse and Kitty raised one delicate hand and waved to him. She was deeply distressed and her heart softened.

'O, Captain Nathaniel – I cannot bear to see him so. Such a great man, the hero of a hundred fights, looking so ill and weak.'

'I fear for his life – only you can save him, Miss Barnes.'

'Then tell him I will do as he wishes.'

Either he had not been so ill as she had been told or her message miraculously revived him, for arrangements for the wedding then went ahead with amazing speed. (It is remarkable to imagine Kitty telling this story to the House of Lords some fifty years after these extraordinary events when she was a widow in her late sixties, but that is how it has survived, recorded in the pages of *Hansard*.)

Kitty's aunt helped her to prepare for the long journey and on the evening of 6 August 1812 Thomas came to the house with a carriage. Her maid, Anne Moxham, accompanied them inside the carriage, while Cochrane's servant, Dick Carter, rode outside. There was a strange feeling of unreality about it all, yet once she had agreed to the elopement she felt no fear, and Thomas, despite his recent illness, was in the best of spirits. It was dark for the first part of the journey and on and on they travelled, stopping only to change horses, taking whatever animals were available, sometimes four and sometimes two.

Through the night and all the next day, the carriage sped on its way, the countryside rolled by. Another night came and by this time, Kitty was very tired, sometimes she slept a little and sometimes Thomas dozed beside her. When they changed horses she stepped out of the carriage and entered the posting house to attend to her toilet. They would have a quick meal and then on they went again. It was almost two days later, on the afternoon of 8 August when they crossed the border into Scotland.

'That's Gretna Green,' Thomas said, with impulsive joyous laugh. 'Thank God we are all right. Mouse – we are over the border. We shall soon be there.'

'Are we to be married in Gretna Green?' she asked.

'No. We shall stay at the Queensberry Arms at Annan. Moxham, when we arrive you are to get a comfortable room for Lady Cochrane.'

He turned to Kitty, looking so happy that she could not help smiling back and snapped his fingers in the air with a triumphant gesture. 'You are mine now, and you are mine forever!' he declared.

It was evening when the carriage finally stopped by the door of the inn. Stiff from the long, jolting journey Kitty stepped out of the carriage and entered the inn on the arm of Lord Cochrane. Almost at once he seated himself at a table, just as if he had been at home, and began writing. Kitty sat waiting, watching, looking around her in some surprise, still wondering about this strange wedding. She had known it would be different from the grand ceremony in church she had dreamed of but she had no idea how simple it was, in fact, to be. Presently Thomas looked up from his writing.

'Dick,' he called. His servant stepped forward. 'Tell Moxham to come here, will you?'

Kitty's servant had gone to see that a room was ready for her mistress. Then Thomas turned to Kitty and handed the pen and paper to her.

'I want you to copy what I have written and mind you write it carefully.'

Slowly and clearly, in her best handwriting, as if it had been in her copybook at the school she had so recently left and taking much longer over it than Thomas had done, Kitty wrote. When she had finished she looked up at Lord Cochrane. She could read the excitement in his face and he glowed with happiness as he read it over.

'Dick.' He beckoned his servant to step nearer. 'I came here to be married – and this lady –' he bowed gallantly in Kitty's direction – 'is my wife. Be so good as to read that paper and sign it.'

Dick Carter did as he was instructed, then Lord Cochrane turned to Anne Moxham and bade her to do the same. Anne glanced in Kitty's direction and she nodded her assent.

'Thank you. Now you may go.'

As soon as the servants had left the room Thomas jumped up from his seat at the table, lifted his hands in the air and began to dance a sailor's hornpipe.

'Now Mouse – you are mine. Mine for ever,' he chanted as he danced about the room, irrepressible in his happiness.

'I don't know, Thomas –'

'What don't you know, Mouse?'

'Well, I have had no parson or church. Is this really the way they marry in Scotland?'

'Oh, yes,' he said. 'You are mine, sure enough. You cannot get away.' He danced over to her. 'You must trust me. I know what I am doing.'

He took her in his arms and kissed her until her doubts subsided. She loved and trusted him completely and accepted that the irregular wedding was as legal and binding as he assured her it was. She little knew what great anguish and trouble it was to cause her in later life.

They had only a short time together for almost at once Thomas said, 'I have no time to spare. I must be back in London for my uncle's marriage.'

'I did not know your uncle was about to be married also.'

'Yes, it is on the 11th or 12th, I forget which, but I wish to be there as if nothing had happened. Remember, this marriage is our secret, Mouse.'

'Just as you wish.'

'I have given instructions to Dick and he will bring you back to London as soon as he can.'

The inn seemed drab and dull after he had ridden away. Nothing had been as Kitty had expected it to be on her wedding day. She felt tired and aching from the long journey. The landlady came with a lamp to light the way upstairs for her. 'May I have a bath, please?' Kitty asked.

'No, ye cannae. There are nae baths here,' snapped the old lady. Kitty had never heard such a broad Scottish accent before and could scarcely understand what the old woman said. 'Will you bring me some soft water, then?'

'I've had a big wash the day, there's nae watter left.'

Kitty was angry and sad and lonely. She sighed. 'No soft water, nor a bath – what kind of place do you call this?'

'It's the Queensberry Arms at Annan,' replied the cross old woman.

Kitty soon returned to London and though for a time the marriage was kept secret, it was not long before Basil Cochrane discovered the truth. He lost no time in carrying out his threat to disinherit his rebellious nephew, but characteristically Thomas snapped his fingers at his uncle and found a house for himself and Kitty. It was called Holly Hill and it was situated in Hampshire.

He returned to his battles in Parliament, campaigning against those whom he felt had made money out of the war at the expense of the sailors; because he fought the Establishment, he made enemies. Kitty's first son was born in April 1814. Only a few months later, her husband was convicted of fraud and sentenced to one year's imprisonment. He was accused of starting a rumour of Napoleon's defeat which had repercussions on the Stock Exchange and he was supposed to have benefited from this. Kitty was furious! Never for one moment could she believe he would be capable of such a thing! Passionately she defended his name to anyone who would listen as she waited for his release, but she was not the only one who believed in him. On his conviction a writ was moved for a by-election at Westminster, but at a mass meeting his constituents resolved unanimously that Lord Cochrane was innocent and was a fit and proper person to represent them. His name was proposed and he was re-elected with a roar of approval.

His sentence still had three months to run when to Kitty's amazement her husband arrived home. Her delight was tempered by concern at the realisation that he had been injured, and as she fussed around him, she heard how for months he had been plotting to escape. Because the rooms in which he was confined in the King's Bench Prison were so high it had been considered unnecessary to put bars at the windows. Outside was a sheer drop to the prison yard and beyond that was a high outer wall, topped with spikes. It stood higher than the windows but not more than twelve feet away. Dick Carter, Thomas Cochrane's faithful servant, managed to smuggle in to him some small lengths of rope, hardly thicker than stout cord.

Thomas had waited until after midnight, when the warders were furthest away on their rounds, then carrying the coiled rope, he climbed out of the window, and scaled up to the roof. From there he could look down on the spiked wall. Despite the darkness he threw a running noose over the spikes and made fast the other end to the prison roof. Hand over hand he made his way along the thin rope down to the outer wall. Perched there between those vicious spikes, he paid out another length of rope and began his descent. With twenty feet still to go, the rope broke. He fell heavily and lay unconscious for a considerable time. Luckily no bones were broken, and although he was badly bruised and sprained he managed to crawl to the house of an old servant.

Kitty urged him to hide, especially when she learned that a reward of three hundred guineas had been offered for his capture. There was a great hue and cry in London and though many of his neighbours knew of his presence, not one of them would stoop to denounce him, even to claim such a reward. He had his own plans, however, for Thomas Cochrane was not a man to skulk in corners. He stayed at home for only a few days, just long enough to recover from his injuries. Then he went boldly to London and attempted to take his place in the House of Commons. But it was a futile gesture and his appearance there was short-lived. A Bow Street Runner and some tipstaffs were sent for and after a sharp and undignified scuffle, Cochrane was carried out of the chamber and back to prison. There he was thrown into a dank, airless dungeon where his health was so greatly impaired that before long he had to be moved to better rooms until his release.

In the next two years the Cochranes' financial position grew worse and worse and although Kitty tried to economise, there was little she could do to help. By the spring of 1817, Cochrane's creditors succeeded in getting a court order on their house but Thomas refused to move and Kitty prepared to fight with him. At one time the Sherriff and twenty-five constables laid seige to the house but Thomas let it be known that he had placed bags of explosives at strategic positions, and that he and the servants were armed. In truth, the 'bags of explosives' held only charcoal, but the constables had heard enough of the exploits of this extraordinary man to take his warning seriously. A month later one of the officers managed to slip in through an open window into the house where Thomas was caught at breakfast, and there was nothing he could do but admit defeat. With a characteristic gesture he snapped his fingers and arranged to leave the house. But at once he began to plan another adventure.

Kitty became pregnant again and their second son, Horace William, was born in March 1818. At about that time Thomas accepted an assignment to take command of the navy in Chile, which was fighting for independence from Spain. Kitty was determined to accompany her husband to South America but before they left England, her uncle, John Simpson, now living in Fairborn in Kent, had a serious talk with both of them.

'It worries me that you have never been properly married in church,' he said. 'South America is a Catholic country, and the people there are bound to attach great importance to church ceremonies. Suppose anything were to happen to you, Thomas, and Kitty was left alone with the children—'

'Heaven forbid!' murmured Kitty.

'Amen to that. But you are going into active service again, and it is my duty to think of Kitty's welfare. She should have a proper marriage certificate. A clandestine Scottish wedding will mean nothing to those foreigners.'

'If it will put your mind at rest, I have no objection,' said Thomas. 'Though I assure you that Kitty and I are as properly and legally married as any couple in the world.'

Thomas was very upset however when, on approaching the parson he discovered that in the words of the service, it would be necessary for him and Kitty to be designated as 'bachelor' and 'spinster'!

'What rubbish! We are man and wife – have been for the past six years, and we have two sons to prove it.'

But Kitty's aunt and uncle continued to voice their fears. They were so genuinely distressed because she had no marriage lines, that at length he agreed. On 22 June 1818 Kitty and Thomas were married once more, as 'bachelor' and 'spinster' in the church of Speldhurst in Kent. Less than two months later, they sailed away in an open fishing smack bound for Boulogne. From there they embarked on the *Rose*, and started on the voyage that took them round Cape Horn to Valparaiso. Three days before Christmas of that year, Lord Cochrane took up his appointment as Admiral and Commander in Chief of the Chilean Navy. His flagship was a 50-gun frigate once the *Maria Isabella* because it had been recently captured from the Spanish and renamed *The O'Higgins* after General Bernardo O'Higgins, leader of the movement for self-government, whose Irish father had been the Spanish Viceroy of Peru.

Kitty Cochrane enchanted the Chileans with her beauty and force of character. On one occasion, having just come ashore from a voyage in *The O'Higgins*, she rode into the town of Huacho where the troops were being inspected in the square. Afterwards Lt Col Miller, who was there, wrote, 'The sudden appearance of youth and beauty, on a fiery horse, managed with skill and elegance, absolutely electrified the men! They had never before seen an English lady. *"Qué graciosé! Que guapa! Es an angel del cielo"* (How graceful! How beautiful! An angel of heaven!) were exclamations that escaped from one end of the line to the other.'

'This is our general!' shouted Miller, joining in the enthusiasm.

Kitty turned her sparkling eyes towards the men and bowed graciously and as she turned her horse and cantered away, they all, officers and men cheered, *'Viva! Viva!'*

Naturally Kitty was always anxious when her husband was away fighting great sea-battles against the Spanish fleet. Whenever possible she took the children to see him off. On one such occasion she had just taken leave of Thomas and had been ferried ashore, when the final gun boomed out from *The O'Higgins* to summon all hands for sailing. For a moment her attention was distracted from the children and when she looked around for little Thomas, she realised he was no longer with her. To her horror she saw that somehow her son was with some sailors in the last boat out! He was only five years old and he was waving his cap and shouting *'Viva la Patria!'* to everyone's great amusement – except Kitty's. There was no alternative but for Lord Cochrane to take him on the voyage. They were away for six months.

Kitty heard later how the sailors made him their mascot and cut out a set of midshipmen's clothes for him. When the ship sailed into action Cochrane locked his son into his stern cabin, but young Thomas had no intention of missing the excitement and climbed out of the window as the salvoes howled over the ship. To his father's dismay, he appeared on the quarterdeck in the middle of the action and began to make himself useful by handing powder to the gunners for their quarterdeck guns. A Spanish cannon ball hissed across the deck killing the sailor next to the child, and spattering him with blood; but at every attempt to send or even to carry him below, young Thomas howled and kicked so violently that in the end he had to be left. He seemed to live a charmed life during the whole cruise.

In addition to a house in Valparaiso, the Cochranes had a delightful country residence in Quillots. There, one night when Thomas was at sea, an intruder broke in and entered the room where Kitty was relaxing. He brandished a stiletto and demanded that she hand over the secret orders which her husband had left.

'No. I shall give you nothing,' replied Kitty.

She snatched up a paper that lay on her desk and the man grabbed her. Kitty shouted for the servants and she struggled with the ruffian but before help arrived she had been severely cut by his knife. The servants closed in on him and dragged him away; he was locked up and tried and an order was given that he should be executed without the last offices of the Catholic religion. The evening after sentence was passed, Kitty was awakened by a loud wailing beneath her window. She called for the servants and sent them to find out the cause. It was the wife of her assassin, and when the woman was brought in she fell on her knees before Kitty, imploring that her husband should be allowed to have confession and absolution. Her wretchedness moved Kitty.

'I will do all I can,' she promised.

Next morning she pleaded with the authorities, not only for the man to receive the sacraments but to save his life and at last they agreed to commute his sentence to banishment for life.

Time and again Kitty proved herself to be a women of great character. Once when important despatches had to be delivered she took them herself, riding on the back of a mule. The track lay via the celebrated Ponte del Inca, a pass 15,000 feet above sea-level, and because it was October there was deep snow, which held up her progress for a time. With her servants and guide she had to stay for several days in a mountain hut, where she slept on a couch of dried bullock's hide, until the weather conditions improved enough for her to finish the journey down to Mendoza.

While Thomas Cochrane was blockading the port of Callao in February 1821, Kitty visited her friend, the Marchioness de la Pracer, at Quilca. Her youngest son had been unwell and Kitty hoped the change of air might be beneficial to him. The Marchioness placed her palace and every luxury at Kitty's disposal and even arranged a ball in her honour. During these festivities a message came that Spanish soldiers were advancing on Quilca with the object of taking Kitty and her child hostage. Secretly she slipped away from the Ball, changed her dress and made arrangements for horses to be brought to the door, one carrying a special litter for the sick child.

She set out with her faithful servants and travelled all night and into the following morning, until they came to a swollen river. The bridge across it was made only of strips of hide with sticks for the footway and two more lengths of hide which acted as handrails. It was impossible to take the horses over – and on such a bridge an inexpert pedestrian could easily start it vibrating dangerously. At that moment, the bugles of their pursuers were heard. Kitty snatched up her child and ran on to the bridge. By the time she reached half way, it was swaying so violently that she had to stop helplessly, and fell down, clutching her baby, while the decking rippled and the whole bridge swung crazily over the foaming torrent.

'Lie still, Señora,' called one of the servants, Pedro Flores. And Kitty nerved herself to do as she was told till the bridge ceased swaying. Then carefully – slowly – Pedro crawled towards her. The ropes were only intended to take the weight of one person at a time, and at any moment could snap, dashing them all to certain death. Pedro advanced till he could take the child from her, then guided her across. As soon as all their party had crossed they cut the ropes of the bridge which fell into the chasm below.

Sometimes Kitty stayed on board *The O'Higgins* with Thomas. She was there when news came that a Spanish ship loaded with treasure from Callao was about to attempt to escape. If she got clear there would

Jim Jackson was at a party one evening and an Englishwoman rushed up to him saying, 'Ah, at last I see a man who wears a kilt! Do you always wear a kilt?'

He told her about his job as guide at the Gretna Green Blacksmith's Shop. 'Then the lady brought her daughter over to meet me, because she had just been married in Annan that afternoon. They hadn't realised that every day we do anvil ceremonies for real brides and grooms, after they've been to the Register Office. That's the legal one,' Jim says, with a dramatic pause, 'but over the anvil is the wedding of the heart.'

The next morning the whole party went to the Blacksmith's Shop and the young couple took part in the anvil ceremony before leaving for their honeymoon. Afterwards both sets of parents reaffirmed their vows to each other over the anvil in Jim's special anniversary ceremony. It was a happy occasion for all – including Jim.

---

be no hope of overtaking her and so Thomas set sail immediately; there was not even time to send Kitty ashore. When *The O'Higgins* sailed in to attack, Kitty remained on deck. She was standing so close to one of the ship's guns that the gunner hesitated, uncertain whether he should fire the piece so near to his Admiral's delicate lady. Kitty seized the man's arm and directed the burning match to fire the gun. The explosion deafened her and as the iron cannon rolled back on its wooden track, Kitty fainted. She was carried below but when she appeared on deck at the end of the engagement, the whole crew of *The O'Higgins* sang their Chilean national anthem in her honour. It was her last experience of war. She returned to England soon afterwards, partly for her health and partly to watch over her husband's interests at home.

In two and a half years Admiral Cochrane had made Chile mistress of her own waters and her flag became respected from Cape Horn to Panama. When he returned to Britain, Thomas and Kitty were married yet again. A relative, Sir Robert Preston, decided to bequeath his estate in Culross to Lord Cochrane, but he insisted that they be married according to the Church of Scotland.

'I have already married my wife twice,' laughed Thomas, when this was suggested to him, 'but I am so well satisfied I have no objection if I marry her twenty times!'

Their third wedding was in Edinburgh on 18 October 1825. Lord Cochrane succeeded to the title of Earl of Dundonald in 1831 and after many more adventures he died in Kensington in 1860. He was so greatly honoured that he was buried in Westminster Abbey. That was when the problems over their marriages began.

Kitty, Lady Dundonald, was then in her sixties and living in France. She had four sons and one daughter. Young Thomas, who as a little boy had sailed into battle on *The O'Higgins*, expected to succeed to the title. This was contested by the third son who pointed out that their parents had been described as 'bachelor' and 'spinster' at their marriage in Kent, and this suggested that the first two sons were illegitimate. It was a matter for long debate in the House of Lords, until they called Lady Dundonald to give evidence before them.

Kitty did so on 24 July 1862, fifty years after Thomas had carried her over the border for their clandestine first wedding. Kitty left their lordships in no doubt, as she told them vividly and clearly the full details of her three weddings. As she finished the chamber rang with her words of praise, 'My husband was a glory to the nation in which he was born – the most honourable man I have ever known. I loved him.'

CHAPTER SEVEN

# Ellen Turner and Edward Gibbon Wakefield

One of the worst scandals in the history of Gretna Green was the abduction of Ellen Turner, a schoolgirl, not quite sixteen years of age. The details were given wide press coverage at the notorious trial that followed, and the events were so extraordinary that they read like a Victorian melodrama.

The drama began on 7 March 1826, at the Misses Daulby's Seminary for the Daughters of Gentlefolk, just outside Liverpool. That morning, as she dressed in the dormitory of her exclusive boarding-school, Ellen Turner had no idea that the following day she would be married at Gretna Green. How could she know? She had not then met her future bridegroom. She was pretty, intelligent and said to be of an amiable disposition; she was also the daughter of a very rich mill-owner, William Turner, Sheriff of Cheshire.

From the court records it is clear that, with the other girls at school, Ellen often dreamed of romance. Marriage was the only career for which girls of her class in society were prepared, and Ellen loved to read stories of romantic elopements. She often imagined being swept off her feet, of a handsome lover who was waiting for her, but when Miss Daulby sent for her on that fateful Tuesday, Ellen could not in her wildest dreams have imagined the events in which she would soon be involved.

'I fear I have some bad news for you, my dear,' Miss Daulby told her as gently as she could. 'I have received a communication from your home. Apparently your mother has been taken ill and she wishes you to return there to be with her.'

'Oh, poor Mama! What is the matter with her?'

'This letter is from Dr Ainsworth and he asks me not to tell you, but I believe you should be prepared, Ellen, as it seems to be rather serious. Your dear Mama has been stricken with a sudden paralysis.'

When holiday-makers from New Zealand look at one of the old registers of Gretna Hall, which is kept open at the page with the entry of the marriage of Edward Gibbon Wakefield to Ellen Turner, they are absolutely amazed. A common comment is – 'They never told us that in our history lessons at school!'

Ellen gasped. Though she had been partly prepared for such news – Mrs Turner had been unwell for some time – she had never expected it would be so bad.

'I must go to her at once.'

Miss Daulby inclined her head. 'I have already given orders for your things to be packed. I would send my sister with you as a companion on the journey, but Dr Ainsworth suggests that it would be more convenient for you to travel alone. You are sure you will be all right, Ellen?'

'Oh yes, Miss Daulby. Pray do not worry on my account.'

Less than half an hour later Ellen was ready for the journey. A barouche waited at the door and as she went out to it, she noticed that it was not one of her father's carriages. She was a little surprised too, that the manservant who held open the door was unknown to her.

He was quick to explain. 'My name is Thevenot, Mademoiselle.' He had a French accent and a manner that was impeccably plausible and respectful. 'Your father has recently engaged me as butler, ready for the move to the new house.'

Ellen, of course, knew of the mansion her father was having built. To Miss Daulby, Thevenot said, 'You may be assured Mr Turner would not have sent me to fetch the young lady if he was not entirely sure I should take the utmost care of her during the journey. Now we must make all possible speed, for we are to pick up Dr Hill in Manchester.'

Anxious to reach her mother's side as soon as possible, Ellen bade farewell to Miss Daulby and stepped into the carriage. Thevenot swung himself up into the rumble seat behind and away they sped at a rate of twelve miles an hour.

In Manchester the carriage stopped at the Albion Inn to change horses and Ellen was invited to alight and was shown into a private room. There she saw a handsome man, about thirty years of age, dressed in the very height of fashion, who swept a gallant bow as she entered the room. He had a high forehead, crowned with curly brown hair and sideburns that framed his otherwise clean-shaven, strong masculine features.

'Your servant, Miss Turner.' His voice was warm and musical, the smile he gave her was reassuring and his manner was both friendly and courteous. He treated her like a young lady rather than as a schoolgirl, so that Ellen was quite enchanted.

'The carriage will be ready in a moment,' he assured her. 'Please sit down – can I get you anything to eat or drink?'

'No, thank you, Sir.'

He had not told her his name and though she wondered who he was and why he was there, his presence was no more strange than any of the other happenings of the day.

'I trust you had a good journey?'

'Yes, thank you,' replied Ellen , 'though it has been raining very hard for most of the time.'

'The wet weather for which Manchester is indeed famous,' smiled the young man.

Ellen was about to ask him if he knew why she has been sent for in such a hurry, but before she could form the question he had walked to the window and was pointing to a clock which could be seen across the street.

'Do you not think that clock is one of the strangest you have ever seen?' he asked.

Ellen looked but could not see anything particularly remarkable about it. However, she did not like to be impolite since it appeared to arouse so much interest in her companion; he continued to talk about it, as if it were a clock of considerable importance. There seemed to be no opportunity for her to ask him any of the questions that came into her mind as to why they were there together, in the private room at the inn. A few minutes later a serving girl came to tell them the horses had been changed and the carriage was ready.

'Come, Miss Turner. Let us proceed.' The gentleman tucked her hand through his arm, and escorted her down the stairs in a manner that made her feel, not simply grown up, but gave her the heady sensation that he found her quite enchanting. They paused together in the foyer to bid farewell to the landlady, then he escorted her outside. A little crowd of people had gathered around the door, the poor and homeless stared at them and held out begging hands, but Ellen's escort hustled her past protectively and stepped into the carriage with her.

Observing that the horses' heads were not turned in the direction of her father's home at Shrigley, she asked, 'Which way are we going?'

'I will tell you in a moment.' He leaned out of the window and called to the postboys – 'Drive on.' Then he settled back in his seat.

The horses' hooves clattered on the cobbles, the iron-shod wheels rumbled as, with all possible speed, the carriage threaded its way through the city streets and out to the open countryside.

71

Margaret Bunyeon was told by her fiancé that he had made arrangements for their wedding only twenty minutes before they were due to arrive at the Register Office. She thought they were just going on holiday together to Belgium.

Edward Busst and Margaret lived only two doors away from each other in Dunfermline. They had been engaged for more than a year, but when it came to planning the wedding she was very nervous. Edward felt she would have found it too much of a strain to have a big formal ceremony, so he made all preparations in secret.

'I wondered why we were travelling via Gretna,' Margaret said. 'Then I saw my family waiting outside the Register Office.'

Immediately before the wedding Edward presented Margaret with a dress he had designed himself and had specially made for the occasion.

'Miss Turner – do you know why you have been sent for from school?'

'Yes. Miss Daulby thought it proper that I should know, though she was desired not to tell me, that my mother is ill.'

'No. That is not the truth of the matter.' Ellen looked at him in alarm, but he went on hastily, 'I can assure you first of all that, as far as I am aware, your mother is in perfectly good health.'

'But the letter? Miss Daulby – ?' Ellen look enquiringly at her companion and his smiling face, his pleasant manner, his obvious air of breeding and gentility, were all reassuring.

'I had reasons for deceiving Miss Daulby, and you shall have a full explanation bye and bye. Meanwhile just trust me.'

'Oh, I am so glad that dear Mama is not really ill!'

'You may be absolutely assured on that point, as I have already said, Miss Turner.' She smiled. It was a great relief to hear such good news and as the carriage sped through the countryside, her companion made a most flattering effort to please and amuse her. Before long Ellen found herself responding, laughing and enjoying herself a great deal more than she would have done in lessons at school. He talked on all manner of subjects, from the gravest to the most ridiculous, of important and of trifling matters. He was at great pains to please her and he complimented her on her sharp wit and her beauty. There was no doubt in her mind that he was a man who moved in the best society, in Paris as well as London.

At length he asked her, 'Do you know where you are going?'

'No, but I suppose you do?' She laughed as she said it, youthful in her complete trust. 'Indeed I do not think I wish to be told, I rather enjoy the uncertainty.'

'Nevertheless I will tell you. I am escorting you to Yorkshire and we will probably meet your father at Huddersfield.'

'You are a friend of my father's?'

'Indeed I am. My name is Edward Gibbon Wakefield.'

At Huddersfield there was no sign of Mr Turner. The carriage stopped at an inn there and Ellen alighted and went inside. Somehow she was neither surprised nor alarmed when Mr Wakefield told her that her father's plans had been changed, and he suggested that they should drive on through the night towards Kendal, in the hope of meeting up with him there.

'By all means, Mr Wakefield,' Ellen replied, quite willingly.

Never in all her young life had she taken part in such an adventure. To travel through the night in a carriage was not at all the sort of thing a young lady in her circumstances ever did – let alone with such pleasant company. It was strange to think that only that morning she had been in Miss Daulby's Seminary; that there the girls would all be safely tucked into their beds. How they would envy her when she told them about it! It was morning when they reached Kendal and stopped at an inn. Again Ellen was shown into a private room.

'I had hoped that your father would be here,' said Mr Wakefield, 'so he could tell you himself, but I fear now I must break some news to you, Miss Turner.'

'Mama—?'

'No. As I said, your Mama is quite well. My news concerns your father's business. You know he kept his money with the bank of Danby and Kyle at Macclesfield?' She nodded.

'I wish I did not have to tell you this – but it must be done. The bank has failed, and your father has lost everything.'

Ellen gasped.

'My uncle,' Mr Wakefield went on, 'who is a banker in Kendal, lent your father £60,000 which partly relieved him of his debts, but unfortunately in the past few days another bank in Blackburn has also failed. Your father is completely ruined.'

Ellen was quite bewildered; only the term before a friend of hers had been taken away from Miss Daulby's Seminary for exactly the same reason. She had often heard tales of rich and substantial men whose businesses suddenly collapsed but she never dreamed that such a calamity could happen to her Papa.

'How dreadful! Oh, Mr Wakefield, just before I returned to school this term, Papa said he only hoped he could continue to pay the fees. I thought he was joking – we both laughed about it, I had no idea that he really meant it. Poor Papa! If only I could do something to help him.'

'There is a possibility. I told you my uncle is willing to help if it is at all possible. You know your father's solicitor?'

'Mr Grimsditch.'

'That's right. He has hit upon a plan that could make everything right. Settlements could be drawn up and some of your father's property could be transferred to you.'

'And then I could give it back to Papa?' Ellen said eagerly.

'Not quite, because you are under age. But when you marry that property would belong to your husband.'

'But I have no thought of marrying yet.'

'Mr Grimsditch proposes that I should marry you.'

Ellen caught her breath, astonished at such a proposal.

'I told him I could not agree to such a proposition, as I did not even know you, but my uncle insisted that we should meet.' He took her hand and smiled gently at her. 'Now indeed I could assure him that I would be delighted to agree that we should be married. It only remains for you to give your answer.'

'I – I don't know what to say, Mr Wakefield. I – I shall have to speak to my father.'

'And so you shall, my dear. I will go and see if I can find any news of him.'

Ellen was alone for only a short while. When she heard the door opening again she jumped to her feet, ready to throw herself into her father's arms.

'Papa –'

It was another young man who came into the room with Edward Wakefield.

'Miss Turner, this is my brother, William. He has just come from your father.'

'How is he?'

'Mr Turner was very distressed not to be able to meet you here. He has had to go on to Carlisle, and he asks us to escort you there.'

At once all three set off in the carriage, and at Carlisle they stopped at the Bush Inn. William Wakefield went into the inn to investigate and came back with the terrible news that Mr Turner was indeed there, concealed in a small back room, afraid to come out because the bailiffs had surrounded the place.

'You have seen Papa? I must go to him—'

'No. You would be recognised and that would make more trouble for him. He has made two attempts to cross the border, but he could not get away.'

'What can we do then?'

'Only you can save him, Miss Turner,' said William. 'Your Papa begs
you, if you ever loved him, to accept at once my brother's proposal of
marriage.'

Edward Wakefield took her trembling hands in his. 'Do not be afraid,
Miss Turner. I realise this is all very sudden but I promise you our
marriage shall be in name only, until I have taught you to love me.' His
face was gentle, though there was a twinkle of excitement in his eyes.
'And that I surely shall do before long – if you will only agree.'

Ellen knew little of business affairs, but she had read enough
romances to believe that in such circumstances a dutiful daughter must
not hesitate to sacrifice herself to save her father from ruin and disgrace.
Apart from which, this man who was asking to marry her was no
dastardly old villain but the most charming man she had ever met.

'I will do whatever you say, Sir,' she agreed.

'Then let us continue our journey and make for Gretna Green where
we can be married with the minimum of delay.'

They drove through the mountains of Westmorland, and Mr Wakefield suggested that some summer they should pass a few days in that
delightful countryside. With the promise of such future pleasures,
Ellen's spirits were high, and seeing herself in the role of noble heroine
was quite a heady sensation. They began to discuss the novels of Sir
Walter Scott and as they approached the border, talked merrily of
elopements and of the hair-breadth escapes of runaway couples.

'Won't it be a surprise to everyone at home in Cheshire when they
hear that I am married!' Ellen exclaimed.

'The wedding service is quite a simple one, I believe,' said Mr
Wakefield.

'I've read it often in my prayer book,' Ellen said, 'though I little
thought I should take part in it so soon.'

75

The carriage took them to Gretna Hall. They entered a pleasant room, where a fire blazed cheerfully. Ellen waited with anxious excitement as Mr Wakefield spoke to the landlord and made arrangements for the wedding. A 'priest' was sent for and when he arrived he was a very old man, wearing a black coat and velvet waistcoat with breeches of the same colour. On his head was a broad-brimmed hat, like a cleric's. He wore an expression of quiet gravity and had a quaintness of phraseology which Ellen thought rather droll. It was David Lang.

Ellen stood beside Edward Gibbon Wakefield and in the 'marriage room' of the Hotel they went through the service. She gave her answers steadily, thinking how pleased her father would be when he heard how dutifully she had behaved. The ring Mr Wakefield placed upon her finger was rather large and when, the ceremony being over, he turned to her and took her in his arms, she raised her face for his brief kiss.

No sooner was the marriage certificate filled in and signed, the 'priest' and the landlord paid, than Ellen and her new husband were off again. They stopped at a posting inn to dine, then drove south to London. Ellen had had no sleep at all the previous night and was so tired, she could stay awake no longer. But even in London there was little rest, for within a day Mr Wakefield declared he had to be in Paris for some urgent business the following week, so they must move on at once to Dover.

Several times Ellen asked for news of her father, but she was merely told that all was now well with him and that she had no cause to worry. Then they boarded the packet boat and crossed the Channel to Calais, where they stayed at the Hotel Quillac. As he had promised, Edward Wakefield booked separate rooms for them and though he was always tender and courteous towards her, he treated her more like a cherished young sister than a wife.

Together they went to a jewellers and he brought her a new wedding ring to replace the large one that had been used at Gretna. She knew that before they left England, Edward had written to her Papa to tell him of their marriage. From Calais they both wrote to Ellen's parents and she was enchanted when he allowed her to read part of what he had written – 'My dear little wife is an excellent creature and promises to be the delight of my life.' Ellen was able to assure her mother that she was well and happy and she signed her letter 'Ellen Wakefield'.

Edward was always so cheerful, and could easily make light of any obstacles, that she really was happy – except she missed her parents and friends. Then, just one week after the marriage, on 15 March 1826, as Ellen was getting ready to go out for a walk with her husband, there came a knock on the door of her room.

'Who is it?'

'It is Edward – and I have here two of your uncles from England.'

At once Ellen opened the door and threw herself into her uncles' arms kissing them as she always did. She was overjoyed to see those familiar, loving faces – then she realised her uncles were not alone. Behind them were some strangers.

'I'm so happy to see you,' cried Ellen. 'But tell me – how are my dear Papa and Mama?'

'Your Mama is very ill.'

'But you said – ?' She turned to Mr Wakefield, unable to understand.

'Mrs Turner was in perfectly good health when you left Liverpool, as far as I knew.'

'It is the distress of losing you, my dear Ellen, that has brought on your mother's illness.'

'But I only did what I could to save Papa.'

Sadly the truth of the story came out. Her uncles had not come to Calais alone, with them was a lawyer and several officers from the Bow Street police. Only then did Ellen learn how shamefully she had been deceived. Her distress deepened with every passing moment, as she heard that there had not been one word of truth in any of the terrible things that Mr Wakefield had told her. Her father's affairs were all in good order, nothing had ever been wrong with them. This cruel deception had been perpetrated upon her entirely for Edward Gibbon Wakefield's personal gain.

'You must come home with us without delay, Ellen,' said Uncle Robert.

'Ellen's place is here with me. She is my wife,' protested Wakefield.

'No. You forced her to go through a marriage ceremony, but it was against her will.'

'Did I put any force upon you to marry me, Ellen?'

'You told me that by marrying you, I would save my father from total ruin.'

'That is persuasion, not force. You gave your answers of your own free will, Ellen, did you not?'

'Yes, but – '

'There you are.' He turned triumphantly to the uncles.

'That was no binding marriage. Officers, arrest that man,' commanded Uncle Robert.

'Unfortunately we now stand on French soil. It would be outside our jurisdiction to arrest him.'

'If Mr Turner values his daughter's happiness,' said Edward Wakefield, 'he must drop all these foolish charges. He will find me an excellent son-in-law—'

'That he will never do! He is outraged by your callous abduction of his daughter. I shudder to think what my poor niece has been through with you.'

Edward Wakefield turned to Ellen. 'Please assure your uncles that this is the first time I have entered your bedroom. Tell him we have lived as brother and sister.'

'That is so,' agreed Ellen.

'I should like to have that statement in writting,' said Robert Turner, 'so that I may at least set her parents' minds at rest on that score.'

'Willingly, I assure you she is still a maid. What sort of a monster do you take me for? But the fact remains that she is my wife, and I have no wish to part with her.'

'She shall not stay with you a moment longer. Are you not aware of the distress you have caused her parents? They are both sick with worry and Mrs Turner's condition may even be dangerous.'

'I thought only to help them,' Ellen exclaimed. 'Now I am so confused – I must go home straight away.'

Whereupon Edward Wakefield said, 'Believe me, dear Ellen, I had no idea your mother was so ill. In that case, of course you must go to her at once. I will accompany you, if these gentlemen will assure me that I shall not be arrested when I set foot in England.'

'I cannot answer for that,' said Sergeant Cross. 'Your brother has already been arrested for his part in your crime.'

'Then it seems I must stay here until things can be sorted out. But, Ellen, remember you are still my wife.'

'That farce in Scotland holds no validity within the law. Take off that ring, Ellen, and give it back to him. You need never see this villain again.'

She looked down at the plain gold band and slowly drew it from her finger, then held it out to Edward. He took it from her and the look he gave her was still one of tenderness; 'I shall preserve it carefully,' he said, 'until such time as I can put it back on your finger. Do not think too harshly of me, my dearest little wife.'

'Come Ellen, we must catch the next boat home.'

Ellen returned home with her uncles. She had to tell her story over and over again – to them, to her parents, to the police, to her father's solicitors and also to neighbours and friends, who were agog with the sensationalism of the affair. She heard from them the bitter truth of how shamefully she had been exploited, and of the wicked deceit that had started with the forged letter sent to the school.

It had only been when Miss Daulby discovered that Ellen had not arrived at Shrigley, that a hue and cry had been raised. Mr and Mrs Turner managed to trace her arrival at Manchester and again at

Huddersfield but then the trail had been lost. They had been in despair, having no idea what had happened to their daughter, until they received the letter from Wakefield, written in Carlisle, begging that they would make themselves easy in mind as he had married their daughter. Mr Turner had immediately travelled to London to put the matter into the hands of the police. It was soon discovered that Wakefield and Ellen had left for France, and Mr Turner sent his brothers with the police officers in search of them, carrying a letter from the Prime Minister to the British Ambassador in France. If, during the week Ellen had spent with Wakefield, there had been stirrings of love, it was speedily killed by the denouement that followed.

Edward Gibbon Wakefield's friends advised him to flee to America but he elected to stand trial and returned to England voluntarily, to face the consequences of his folly. The hearing commenced at the Lancaster Assizes when, together with his brother William, he was accused of having 'Feloniously carried away one Ellen Turner, spinster, for the sake of the lucre of her substance; and for having afterwards unlawfully and against her will married the said Ellen Turner.'

Frances Wakefield, stepmother to Edward and William, and the servant Thevenot, were also indicted for conspiracy. Frances Wakefield, it was said, had planned the abduction, having taken it upon herself to procure rich wives for her stepsons. The scheme had been concocted amid the idle and fashionable circle of Paris where, with total lack of restraint or common sense, Edward had gaily promised that he could carry off 'the weaver's daughter'. The three Wakefields pleaded not guilty and applied for a postponement of their trial. Edward was remanded to Lancashire Gaol and while there he wrote this poem:


### A NEW SERENADE

(To the tune of 'Blue Bonnets Over the Border')

Wake! Wake! The carriage is waiting, love,
Down by the grove near the river's green border –
Wake! Wake! Here at your grating, love,
Stands your true lover at Cupid's soft order.
    The horses are champing,
    The post-boys are stamping,
Steal from your slumber, love; all is in order;
    'Tis but a pleasant ride
    O'er the fair countryside –
Hey for the Green that lies over the border.

What though your father may fume, my sweet Ellen,
May grumble, and rave about actions at law;
Like Paris, I'll fly with my sweet English Helen,
And shew I don't value his actions a straw;
  The lawyers may take
  Their retainers, and shake
Their big wigs at the Bar, ranged in terrible order –
  Mount on my pillion
  My maid of a million
A fig for their threats when we drive o'er the border!

Come from your pillow – the morning is shaking
Her tresses of light o'er the brow of the hill;
Like these, in her bloom and her blushes awaking,
And e'en in her coldness, like thee, my love, still
  Steal from your pillow, love;
  Come to the laurel grove,
Let not a footfall alarm your rough warder;
  Trust your coy charms
  To your true lover's arms,
And we'll laugh at them all when we drive o'er the border!

The trial eventually commenced on 23 March 1827, and it was one of the sensations of the year. Ellen herself gave evidence, though the defence objected on the grounds that a wife could not testify against her husband. But the legality of her marriage was obscure, especially as she had been only fifteen at the time it was contracted. *The Times* described her as 'a pretty genteel girl'. The defence made much of her apparent willingness to go through the marriage ceremony.

Edward Wakefield still spoke eloquently of the escapade, saying, 'My great object was to draw her out, to see what sort of mind she had, to learn what had been her education and what were her opinions, manners, habits – a state of high excitement caused my spirits to overflow. She was almost equally elated – instead of having to bring my conversation down to the capacity of an ordinary schoolgirl, I found I could talk at random and that she understood every word. She too was gratified to discover that I enjoyed her display of natural wit and the keen sense of the ridiculous with which she is gifted. Marriages it is said, are made in heaven. Ours was made by the first two hours of our conversation.'

There was, however, little that could be said in the Wakefields' favour. The defendants were all found guilty, the jury retiring only for fifty minutes to consider their verdict. Edward was sentenced to three years imprisonment in Newgate Gaol and William to three years in Lancaster Castle. Though Frances, their stepmother, was found guilty, no sentence was ever imposed upon her and she was freed.

The problem of whether under the law of Scotland, Ellen was or was not Mrs Wakefield was so obscure that it was found necessary to set it at rest by a special Act of Parliament. To the very end Edward spoke strongly against the annulment of his marriage to Ellen but his pleadings were of no avail.

When Edward Gibbon Wakefield began his three year sentence in Newgate, it seemed impossible that he could ever again make a success of his life. But he was no ordinary man. His biographer writes 'it is difficult to imagine how he ever came to think he could succeed in his plan of marrying Ellen Turner. He would certainly have abandoned it, even at the last moment, before telling Ellen the story of the bankruptcy, if it had not been for the strange turn of fate, which ordained that she should seem perfectly content to go with him.

'Ridiculous as it may sound, his abduction of Ellen was to some extent influenced by his desire to become a Member of Parliament for Macclesfield and help to improve the lot of the silk-weavers there. No one of course believed that! There could not have been anyone in the land who was not convinced that money was the dominant motive!' Especially when it was revealed that he was a widower at the time of his marriage to Ellen Turner, and moreover that it was the second time he had made a runaway marriage.

When he was twenty he had fallen in love with Miss Eliza Susan Pattle, the only child of a wealthy East Indies merchant from whom she had inherited everything and who lived with her mother and two elderly uncles. Eliza was not only rich but beautiful and she was a ward in Chancery. There was considerable opposition to her marrying Edward who, though a gentleman, had neither money nor prospects.

The two old uncles were addicted to cock-fighting and Edward, though he normally found cruelty to animals disgusting, pretended an interest in the sport to please the uncles, until they almost began to like and trust him. Almost, but not quite, and they certainly knew that their niece was quite bewitched by him, so Edward formed an ingenious plan to elope with her. He arranged for two carriages to leave Tunbridge Wells, where they lived, at the same time, driving in opposite directions. In one carriage he travelled with Eliza, in disguise, while in the other there were two people dressed to represent them. Just as Edward had hoped, the uncles followed the wrong carriage, while he and Eliza drove to Ipswich without being followed.

They arrived at dead of night at the home of Edward's cousin. Edward managed to enter the house and burst into his cousin's room, where he

Keith and Amanda Brunt came from Belfast for their wedding on 13 June 1988. Neither of them wanted a conventional church wedding and the weeks of nerves and worry that can accompany it. Going to Gretna they decided would be relaxing, and romantic and different – and they really enjoyed their wedding. They told only Mandy's mother and her best friend, Toni – but they were taken by surprise when Toni and her husband and small baby suddenly turned up in Gretna an hour or so before the wedding.

After they had signed the register Miss Bryden disappeared for a moment, then returned with a beautiful bouquet – it was from Keith's brother, who had been puzzled by a few things that had been said and suddenly guessed where they were. He rang the Register Office and checked that Amanda and Keith were on the list for that day and immediately arranged the flowers.

Over the previous weeks they had written letters to all their friends and relatives, to tell them of their wedding, and invite them to a champagne reception on the following Sunday at the home of Mandy's parents. They had a hundred guests, and showed the video – and there wasn't a woman with a dry eye in the house! Mandy wore the wedding dress that had been her mother's and was delighted to have a second occasion on which to dress up in it.

woke him with the words 'I want your boat.' After brief explanations, the cousin came down and Eliza emerged from some bushes where she was hiding. The cousin helped them into the boat, they rowed across the river Orwell, took another chaise and hastened up over the border to Edinburgh where they were married.

Since Eliza was a ward of Chancery, the Lord Chancellor was invoked against Wakefield, but he pleaded so eloquently that he persuaded the Chancellor, not only of the propriety of his marriage, but was also even able to enlist his help to make peace with Eliza's mother. Edward was said to have been devoted to his lovely young wife and the union, though brief, was a very happy one. The marriage improved his financial and social status and he obtained a position with the British Legation in Genoa, where his daughter, Susan Pricilla, was born. Unfortunately Eliza died in 1820, at the birth of their second child, a son.

When Edward Gibbon Wakefield began his three year sentence in Newgate Gaol it was a notoriously unpleasant place. He was horrified by the scene in the chapel on the Sundays before the executions of felons took place; he must have been aware that he could easily have been one of them, for there were many who said he deserved to hang. So, he began to turn his energy to prison reform. One of his cousins was Elizabeth Fry, the renowned social reformer, visited him quite frequently, and her company must have given him much encouragement in this work. In particular, he wrote of four condemned men: a sheep-stealer; a clergyman who had been convicted of forgery; and two petty thieves, one of whom was only eighteen. The paper he wrote was published after his release, and called public attention to the scandalous frequency with which the death penalty was imposed for comparatively minor offences. It was considered to be a remarkable document. One newspaper commented, 'Out of evil comes good, for to Mr Wakefield's three years imprisonment in Newgate we are indebted for this judicious and serviceable publication . . . he has laboured wisely and diligently to atone for the wrongs he committed and every good man will be content to forget that he ever erred'. Another newspater commented: 'The imprisonment of Mr Edward Gibbon Wakefield will probably prove a source of the most essential benefit to the country.'

The paper, *Punishment by Death*, was but the beginning. Wakefield went on to examine the effects of transportation on crime prevention and its impact on the colony to which criminals were sent. He emigrated to Australia, where he did excellent work in connection with the colonisation of that country. He moved on to New Zealand, and later to Canada, and became a respected reformer of the entire British Colonial system. When he died in 1862 Lord Norton said, 'He was a man of genius!'

Ellen's story was not so happy. In 1829, while Edward Wakefield was still in prison, she was married to Thomas Legh of Lyne Park, Chester. He was a respectable businessman who owned a good deal of property in Lancashire. Two years later, still only twenty-one, she died giving birth to a baby daughter. With hindsight it would seem that her innocent intuition to like and trust her dashing abductor had not been entirely misplaced.

# CHAPTER EIGHT

# More Scandals

The trial of Edward Gibbon Wakefield stirred up strong emotions among the general public, which had been rumbling for many years, about the ease with which marriages could be entered into north of the border. There was also considerable feeling that the sentences passed in the courts as a direct result were nowhere near harsh enough. After Wakefield's trial, Lord Tenterden said, 'Three years imprisonment falls very short of the punishment which ought to follow such a crime.' Mr Peel pointed out that hundreds of delinquents, many less guilty than Wakefield, had forfeited their lives. Sir John Cross asserted, 'Had this offence been committed on English ground, instead of at Gretna, in Scotland, two at least of these defendants would in due course of law have been condemned to an ignominious death.' Similarly, a leader writer of the time wrote, 'Seduction exists in this country to a very great extent. The fairer portion of creation enter into friendship more readily and warmly than men. How sweet are the words of those who urge us to do the very things we desire! It is dangerous to play with young ladies' hearts. Some fancy their hearts are tough and bear a deal of pulling about. This is a mistake. They are made of egg shell and are easily crushed.'

Ellen Turner was by no means the youngest bride to be married at Gretna. In May 1815, Captain Bontein of the Guards, a widower of forty-four eloped with a Miss Stanley. She was the daughter of Sir John Stanley, an Indian Chief Justice and was just thirteen years of age. 'Claverhouse' wrote: 'The parties were pursued by Lady Stanley, but the marriage had been accomplished and consumated before her ladyship came up with the runaways. The parties were afterwards reconciled at the Bush Hotel, Carlisle. The main objection was the age of the gentleman as compared with the tender years of the lady.'

Ann Jane Ward was only twelve years of age at the time of her wedding to John Atkinson in 1854. Ann, the daughter of a 'gentleman of

Some years ago a group of young men in Langholm were chatting about girls when one began boasting he could not only take his choice of the village lassies, but that he could marry one that very day if he wanted. The bold statement was challenged and a wager of a bottle of whisky offered and taken.

The young man watched the girls from the factory clattering home in their clogs and waited for the one he knew and fancied. He told her he could no longer live without her and begged her to go to Gretna with him straight away. She agreed, went home and began to bustle around getting ready, and told her mother she was going to marry young B. Then her father came in, and he did not approve either of the boy or of her marrying in such haste and locked the lassie in her room.

The intending husband and his companions waited in the yard of the inn, and when there was no sign of the girl his friends began to taunt him. He decided that his lassie had changed her mind, but pride made him determined to win his bet, so he called on another girl he liked. She accepted and they all set off for Gretna together.

This news soon reached the father of the first girl, who then unlocked the door and told her how lucky she was that she had not married such a fickle man. She did not agree, though she did not tell her father so, and knowing there was a footpath to Gretna, seldom used but shorter, she set out as quickly as she could. The path went over the Solway Moss, thickly covered with heather and brambles. She scrambled over fences and waded through burns and peaty bogs. She was scratched and wet, her shoes were soaked but at last she arrived at Gretna. She saw the wagonette drawn up at the inn and rushed forward.

'I'm here – I'm here! Is the weddin' ower?'

Everyone gazed in astonishment at the bedraggled figure. The 'priest' stood poised, just about to perform the wedding. The lassie's courage and determination won everybody's admiration, and the young man married her. He won his bottle of whisky and the other girl just had to accept it.

fortune, who resided on his own estate at Windermere', was a pupil at the boarding school of Miss Jane Bishop. John Atkinson was the church organist at Appleby, in Westmorland.

In August of that year, according to a report on his trial for abduction at the County Assizes on 12 August 1854, Mr Atkinson 'was engaged by

Miss Bishop to give lessons in music to the young ladies at her establishment'. Before long he was discharged because 'it had been observed that an intimacy had sprung up between him and Miss Ward'. Miss Bishop wrote in his reference that 'she was much obliged to him for the proficiency the young ladies had made in music and would be glad to recommend him'. There was no fault to find in him, she told the court, except 'Miss Ward's overweening partiality for her music tutor'. However, dismissal did not end the friendship. John and Ann began a secret correspondence and on one occasion she sent him a locket. Miss Bishop found out about this and at once wrote and asked him to return it. At first he did not reply but Miss Bishop wrote again and said that if he did not return the locket at once, she would be obliged to put the matter into other hands, as she was responsible for the property of her pupils. John Atkinson then sent back the locket with a note saying it was a pity so small an affair should have caused so much disturbance.

On 24 May, Miss Bishop took her pupils to Ullswater for the day returning at about 10.30 pm. At midnight she checked that Ann was safely tucked up in bed but at about four o'clock in the morning Miss Bishop was awakened by a noise and got up. She found the front door unlocked, but put it down to a servant's carelessness; she fastened it and returned to bed. At seven o'clock that same morning she went to Ann's bedroom, but the child was missing. Almost immediately she suspected that Ann had run away with Atkinson, and went to Mr Bird, the superintendent of police. Together they set off to Gretna in pursuit. At the Sark Tollbar they questioned John Murray, who said a couple answering to their description had been married there that morning between seven and eight o'clock. He showed Miss Bishop the register with the entry.

A young farmer named Brass had driven them to the station at Appleby and had accompanied them to Gretna. They were soon traced and all were taken in charge and escorted to Carlisle where Atkinson was taken before a magistrate and committed for trial. Ann Ward was taken home to her parents in the custody of Miss Bishop and Mr Bird.

Three letters which had been sent by Ann to John were found in his possession and were produced in evidence at the trial. They are remarkably mature for a girl of her age. Bella, referred to in two of the letters, was a housemaid at the school.

Ivy House, Appleby

My dear John – I received your lines, and fully understand what they mean, so I give my consent to all your proposals. It is a great comfort to me to think that at last I have got your heart – a little my way. You never will find me unfaithful, so with kind love,

> Believe me, yours ever affectionately,
> Annie Jane Ward.

Your note gave me such pleasure this morning that I could not take any breakfast. I am so glad you have given up that formal name by which you used to call me, my dear John.

> Ivy House.

My Dearest John – You have no idea of the joy with which I received your letter. You asked me to say one word – I think it will be 'yes' and you asked me to fix the day and way of escape. I shall say next Thursday week, and to get up in the morning and be dressed about seven o'clock, then Bella will leave the front door on the latch. I am to leave it open, to set our tyrant off her guard, and then to slip down the street; but I shall leave you to fix the place where we will meet; but at all events it must be retired. You must not have any misgivings in trying. Open your heart before me. You might have been sure I should be only too happy at your doing so. I should have enclosed another stamp for the one you sent, but old 'Crossy' takes care to keep them herself, and if I ask her for one she will know whom it is for. And now, John when you write to Bella send something to me and say if you accede to my arrangement. And now, with kind and truest love, believe me to be your affectionate, sincere and true, – Annie.
I cannot write safely with anything but pencil.

> Ivy House, Appleby.

My Dear John – I am quite ready to join you at the place you mentioned and will, if it be possible, be with you at a quarter to one on Thursday morning. I think I will not call at your house, as I am not sure where it is, and a mistake might not be pleasant. But I think if I go straight up to Battleborough, and not linger, it would be safer. I have a white dress, but it might arouse suspicion, so I shall just keep on my every day one. I shall set my watch on, with the real time, the night before, so I think we will manage it nicely. You must excuse these bad lines, for they are written very hurriedly,

> And believe me to be, dear John,
> Ever your affectionate and true,
> Annie.

May 21. Do not tell Bella anything about our escape for she does not wish me to go, but I can get away by myself.

The defence made the point that Ann had gone away freely and by her own consent, indeed by the letters she almost seemed to have taken the initiative. He drew the jury's attention to the fact that Ann's appearance was of a young lady of seventeen or eighteen years of age, certainly a great deal older than she really was. He argued, 'It was merely a case of going to Gretna Green, when the impossibility of obtaining consent of parents rendered every other course of bringing about consummation equally impossible.' Moreover, he declared that John Atkinson was of good character.

The prosecution doubted this and insinuated that Atkinson had the reputation of being 'wild and gay' with women. It was pointed out, too, that when she came of age, Ann would inherit £10,000 in her own right. The jury quickly returned a verdict of guilty and the judge sentenced John Atkinson to nine months imprisonment.

Again, such a light sentence provoked considerable criticism, as shown by this leading article: 'We could have wished that the presiding judge had found it possible to make such an example of him as would have deterred other music masters, who enjoy the same opportunities, from taking advantage of their pupils. One thing however, the prisoner did not secure, and that was the approbation of the audience. There was not a man or woman present in court who would not have sincerely and unfeignedly rejoiced had Mr Justice Crowder ordered that a series of periodical whippings should be administered to a man who had so grossly abused his trust. This man however is treated in prison as a first class misdemeanant only and enjoys a room to himself, and all the creature comforts which money can purchase.'

Ann's mother had herself been married at seventeen and, at the time of the trial, was only thirty years of age. It was said that her poor father never recovered from the shock and went mad with grief. Ann was taken to Jersey where she lived for the next three years.

The question as to whether these youthful marriages were valid or not seems to have caused great debate among lawyers. In his book *Scotch Marriages*, published in 1893, F P Walton BA Oxon, Advocate, wrote 'The age at which marriage is lawful is fixed by our law at fourteen for males and twelve for females. It is certainly startling that any boy of fourteen and any girl of twelve may, without any ceremony whatever, contract a marriage by which they are bound to each other for life. It was once doubted whether, if there had been actual cohabitation, a boy even under fourteen could not validly marry. A case was tried where a boy of thirteen had gone through a form of marriage with a woman servant in his father's house, and had afterwards at various times cohabited with her. It was decided however, that he was not married. In England the lawful ages are the same, but if either the man or the woman is under

A couple from Liverpool who were married one afternoon in 1987, went to a pub to celebrate and got rather carried away. There are no licensing restrictions in Scotland and the pubs are open from 11 am to 11 pm. The newlyweds were found late at night, very drunk, throwing beer cans at each other close to the police station. They were taken inside and put into cells for their wedding night – separate of course.

twenty-one his or her parents or guardians have the right of objecting to the marriage.'

In another case where a girl under sixteen ran away without the consent of her guardians and was married in Scotland, a suit was brought into court to annul the marriage. It provoked long legal arguments but in the end it was held that the marriage was valid. In fact, it was not until the passing of the Age of Marriage Act in 1929 that marriage under the age of sixteen was definitely made illegal. Thereafter the question 'Are you over sixteen?' was put to all young couples who rushed to Scotland to marry.

Ann and John Atkinson settled the matter for themselves. As soon as she was of age, John fetched Ann back to Westmorland and married her in accordance with the rites of the Church of England. They lived at Brampton Croft Ends, near Appleby, where John continued to teach music. There was an epidemic of 'blackpox' in that part of the country, which claimed many lives in the years between 1860 and 1870. Sadly, John was one of its victims and his Annie was left with seven children.

There were other cases which, though less publicised because they concerned lesser personages, still caused great concern, especially when they involved payments from the public purse, through the Poor Law. The case of one David Faulds, was typical. He had been brought before the court on a charge of neglecting to support his wife, Mary. He denied the marriage until, pushed by the Overseer, Mary produced her marriage lines and declared on oath that she was married at Springfield by the 'priest' Simon Lang on 13 June 1845. A Witness, Margaret Kirney, stated, 'I was present at the marriage between Faulds and Mary Moore, now Mary Faulds. This is better than nine years since. He was sober. My husband and I were married at the same time. Faulds and Mary Moore went with us to Springfield.' The case continued:

*Faulds:* I was drunk and they left me lying on the side of the road. *(Laughter)*
*Witness:* He was not drunk going, but he was in coming back.
*Faulds:* Did we not get something at the Toddhills?
*Witness:* You were sober when you were married.

Faulds then asserted that his wife had never lived with him.

*Mr Hodgson:* She is your wife and you must maintain her.
*Faulds:* Well she would not come and live with me and I wasn't going to carry her on my back. *(Laughter)*
*Mr Hodgson:* Have you never lived together as man and wife?
*Faulds:* No, not at all.
*Mr Hodgson:* I think Mr Forster, that in order to establish marriage you must prove cohabitation after it.

Mary Faulds was then questioned and said this had taken place but not till two years after the marriage.

*Mr Hodgson:* Is Faulds speaking the truth when he says you left him on the road?
*Mary:* No, sir.
*Witness:* We all came home together.
*Mr Rees:* Was he not drunk?
*Witness:* In coming home he might.
*Faulds:* Yes, it was a terrible wet morning and they left me lying in the dykeback without any cap on. *(Laughter)*
*Mr Hodgson:* I think Mr Forster you ought to carry the case further, I think the marriage should be consummated in Scotland. The Magistrates will again adjourn the case to give you an opportunity of proving that this was a legal marriage, we don't think you have done so today.
*Mary:* We were not five weeks married till he gave our names in church.
*Mr Hodgson:* Then why were you not married?
*Mary:* Because he wished to be married at the Catholic chapel and I did not.
*Faulds:* No, no. I don't belong to that side of the house.

The case was adjourned, but on the following Saturday, Mary proved that David Faulds and she lived together as man and wife; consequently the marriage was held good and he was ordered to maintain his wife. Presumably that lifted the burden from the parish, though one is left wondering what sort of support Mary received from Faulds.

A leading article refering to proceedings at the Carlisle Assizes on 6 August 1854 stated: 'The worst of the criminal cases were two charges

Derek and Janet Kenyon were about to leave their hotel for the Register Office when Derek suddenly thought, 'You haven't got any flowers, Janet. You must have flowers.' He asked for directions to the nearest florist, and headed the car in what he thought was the right direction. He took the wrong road – time was getting late – he put his foot down – and that was when the police spotted him.

As the policeman wrote out the ticket for speeding, he noticed Derek's anxiety and asked what was the problem. Derek explained he and Janet were going to be married in about twenty minutes time and he wanted to buy flowers for her.

'I've still got to write out the ticket for speeding – but I'll see you get there,' the policeman said. 'Follow me.'

With his blue light flashing he drove to the florist's shop, waited while the bouquet was bought, and then led them to the Register Office.

That speeding ticket is now one of their souvenirs, especially treasured because of the name of the place they were stopped, by the Lover's Leap.

of bigamy. Both arose out of that laxity with regard to the marriage tie which so often originates at the statute hirings, and is expanded into a violation of the laws of the land as well as of the laws of chastity by the facilities offered for sham marriages on the other side of the Scottish Border. In one case, a man was married to two different women, in no long period of time, by the keeper of the Sark Bridge Tollbar.

'This person (John Murray) appeared in the witness box with a huge package of register books and a still larger stock of assurance. To him the affair seemed to be one of merriment and fun. He was quite delighted, apparently, with the pungent cross-examination to which Mr Overend subjected him. He, forsooth could not be expected to tell, when engaged in splicing half-tipsy couples whether he had married either of them before or not; he had too much business to do for that; and he boasted that if the call for his disgusting services continued to increase in time to come as of late he should be compelled to keep three or four assistants.

'It was no fun, however, to the wife and children the prisoner deserted, and the woman he, in the second instance deceived and dishonoured or the parish which had to maintain her and her illegitimate child. Mr Justice Wightman, with more gentleness than we expected to see, expressed his regret that such scenes as were described were legal

91

anywhere, and we must say that in these days of reform it is a disgrace to our legislators that a check is not interposed to so fruitful a source of immorality and personal wrong.

'The statute hirings and Scotch marriage laws both stand in need of revision,' the leading article continued. 'The other prisoner appeared very stupid but he was equally wicked. His first wife cheerfully gave her assent to his taking another wife and the woman he married was aware that he had a wife living, but supposed that he was legally entitled to enter into a second arrangement with the consent of his "first love". Her folly saved the offender some months of imprisonment and hard labour. It remains to be seen if he, after he has run the round of the tread wheel, attempts to return to his "first love" though it is doubtful if she will hold out open arms to receive him.'

The Gretna 'priests' appear to have been so secure in the legal aspects of their calling that they were able to go to court confidently and hold their own with the eminent barristers who tried to squash them. David Lang, giving evidence at the trial of Edward Gibbon Wakefield, had not been overawed by the legal fraternity who were bent on showing off their superiority of wit and eloquence. He was over seventy but he held his head high when Mr Brougham questioned him.

'I say, you fellow, how long is it since you were an ostler?' David looked earnestly at the Counsel's face and then replied gravely, 'I never was an ostler – were ye ever ane?'

The old 'priest' caught a chill while travelling to or from the trial as an outside passenger on the coach, and although he conducted a few more marriages until 21 June, he never again enjoyed normal health and died on 2 July 1827. Thomas Hood wrote *An Elegy on David Laing, Esq. Blacksmith and Joiner (without licence) at Gretna Green*. Laing is quite often used as the spelling of his name but it is thought to be less correct than Lang. The poem is very long. This is the last verse:

> Sleep – David Laing! – sleep
> In peace, though angry governesses spurn thee!
> O'er thy grave a thousand maidens weep,
>     And honest postboys mourn thee!
> Sleep, David! – safely and serenely sleep,
>     Bewept of many a learned legal eye!
> To see the mould above thee in a heap
>     Drown many a lid that heretofore was dry!
> Especially of those that, plunging deep
>     In love, would 'ride and tie'!
> Had I command thou should'st have gone thy ways
> In Chaise and pair – and lain in Père-Lachaise.

# CHAPTER NINE

# A Change in the Law

Irregular marriages were never approved by the Church of Scotland, any more then they were by the Church of England. In the seventeenth and eighteenth centuries fines were imposed on parishioners who contracted marriages outside the Church. At that time discipline was very strict in the Scottish Kirk, and some clergy would not marry anyone who was not in full Communion. Until Lord Hardwicke's Act, the law of England had actually been less stringent than that of Scotland, and those who wished for a church wedding, which was denied by their own Church, could cross the border southwards to be married by Episcopalian curates. The Elders of the Kirk did not like this at all, and in 1731 seven couples in Gretna were rebuked for having contracted irregular marriages and each couple was fined half a guinea (52½p).

Elliot had his own views on the behaviour of the Elders of the Kirk when he wrote in his *Memoires*, 'Woe betide the unhappy callant and lassie that may increase and multiply without the aid of kirk or magistrate. The poor girl is summoned to appear with her illicit offspring before the Ministers and Elders, severely examined as to the name of the father and all the circumstances concerning the begetting of it, while outward sanctity serves but as a cloak to cover the corruption within and the Elders, versed in lewdness, subject the poor girl to an examination, revolting to every feeling of decency and humanity. The victim has no power to vindicate herself, unless the father happens to be one of the Elders himself.'

Down the centuries the arguments and accusations for and against the Scottish way of marrying, had built up. Then in the mid-nineteenth century, the steady flow of English people to Gretna became a flood because of the opening of the railway line from Carlisle to Glasgow, with trains stopping at Gretna Junction. It was such a long way from the village that it became known as the 'Canada to Calais', but that was no impediment.

When Border TV Presenter Fern Britton was in Gretna making a programme about the village, she was roped in to act as witness to a young couple about to be married at the Register Office. 'We were filming and they just grabbed me on the street,' she said. 'They were young and very much in love, and they'd told no-one about their wedding. It was very romantic – I was in tears.'

Gretna Junction lies on the English side of the River Sark but one had only to walk beneath the railway bridge and follow the footpath into Springfield. The path meanders across a water meadow grazed short by sheep and cattle alongside the swiftly flowing Sark, which winds, eddies, and gurgles between sandy brown banks. In summer it is shallow enough to wade through, harebells and pink clover bloom and crickets chirp among the ox-eyed daisies on the bank. It reaches the road beside the little hump-backed bridge and you have only to scramble up the grassy slope, cross the bridge and you are in Springfield – in Scotland. When trains were due at Gretna Junction the 'priests' used to wait for the 'fugitive lovers'. Mr Ward, the stationmaster, was very much in command of his domain and he would not allow them on to the platform but insisted that they stand behind the railings, about twelve yards from the trains. They were always dressed in black and, looking suitably grave, stood all in a row. Couples needing their services could have a quick look and make their selection.

A writer of those times says, 'The scene at Gretna was past description. The touting "priests" pulled and tugged at their victims like so many omnibus conductors at an "unprotected female" in London. (A strange analogy, surely?) Every "priest" so-called has a scout lying in wait for fugitives and when he falls in with prey cries – "come along with me where most marriages are performed". Thither the poor simpletons go, just as an ox goes to the slaughter.'

The big annual fair in Carlisle was known as Hiring Day; all the farm labourers and domestic servants who were seeking work in the area assembled there, and masters went along to look them over. Deals were struck for the ensuing year's work, and this usually included board and lodgings, since all household servants and most agricultural workers lived in. Those who looked young, strong and healthy would quickly be snapped up and, having been paid by last year's boss and with the expectation of a living for the year to come, they would have a little money to spend on the revelry of the fair. There were peep-shows, performing animals, freaks, fortune-tellers, strolling players, wrestling bouts, gambling and stalls with food and drink.

It was also a day when working folk arranged to get married, being one of the few holidays any of them had. Carlisle is only about ten miles from Gretna and it is on record that about fifty couples were married every year at Gretna on Hiring Day. It is probable that most of those unions were genuine love matches, but there was also a good deal of drunkenness at the fair and this led to allegations of all sorts of criminal activity, some of which was connected with Gretna Green.

One parson, the Rev Dr Buck, lamented that he knew of instances where a couple had met together for the first time on Hiring Day and 'without previous acquaintance, the men usually partially or entirely drunk and the other not much better, starting off with any gentleman's carriage they could take from the stables, or could hire, travelling to Gretna and there going through some form of marriage, passing through a night of drunkenness, and on the following day, thinking themselves totally unmarried, each going back to their places and both resolved on the next Hiring Day to pursue again a path which had proved so pleasant to them the former time.

'The root of the evil,' Dr Buck continued, 'was in the Carlisle Hirings and if those who had influence were to set their faces against them they might . . . eventually be done away with . . . in this way the masters and mistresses would manage to get better servants, with proper "characters" and therefore increased comfort in their domestic circle'.

Most of the good folk of Carlisle, however, simply blamed Gretna Green for their troubles and on Tuesday 20 May 1856 a public meeting was called by the Mayor and attended in force by the magistrates, clergy and other influential inhabitants. The Mayor, not mincing his words said in his opening address that 'the real object they had in view was to have Gretna marriages put a stop to'. Suggestions of immorality were legion; there were doubts about the seriousness with which some couples entered into their bonds; disgust at the ease with which bigamy could be committed; horror at the thought of young girls being seduced and being carried off by unscrupulous villains. It was impossible to refute the fact that such things did go on, for everyone had read of the trial of Edward Gibbon Wakefield and when such cases came before the courts, every salacious detail was seized upon avidly by the Press for the delight of its readers. The faults of the few cast a blight over the whole picture. Many of these arguments had been voiced about the old Fleet Marriages in London and were trotted out again. Murmurings that the law must be changed grew and grew until there was a clamour of protest, not only in Carlisle, but in many other towns in England.

On the night before her wedding, twenty-five-year-old Marie Barnett tried on her specially made wedding ring – then couldn't get it off! She tried everything from petroleum jelly to putting her hand in a bucket of iced water, but the ring remained firmly on her finger. She was still in her home town of Oldham, time was slipping by and she and her boyfriend, Tony, began to think they wouldn't make it to Gretna for the appointed hour. In desperation she called the fire brigade and chivalrously they came to her rescue. They managed to split open the ring. The couple dashed north – and found the press waiting for them. They were the 500th couple to be married at Gretna in 1984!

Yet still there were people who expressed a strong reluctance to change what they saw as 'the beautiful simplicity' of the Scots form of marriage, which would be spoiled by complicated ceremonies. As it stood it was right for the Scottish people, many of whom had no wish to pay for unnecessary frills. It was also suggested that the Scots had such a horror of illegitimacy that this immediate and private means of regularising a union was both important and beneficial. It was not the Scots who abused the system – it was the flood of English that caused what some saw as a disgusting situation. No one suggested that perhaps the English might be permitted to marry without parental consent before reaching the age of twenty-one, to bring them more into line with the Scots.

The Mayor of Carlisle spoke of the 'fearful amount of seduction, bigamy and bastardy' arising from the Gretna marriages. This was challenged by another speaker, Mr Mounsey, who objected to the inclusion of the word 'bastardy', 'I don't think it can fairly be said to lead to that.'

'Oh yes – most decidedly,' he was contradicted. 'In all cases of bigamy the issue of the second marriage, being void in law, are thus made illegitimate. Therefore it does lead to bastardy.'

A minister of the Church of Scotland was one of the few who spoke in defence of the existing system, 'though as a Scots Minister he felt some unwillingness to obtrude' himself upon the matter. Nevertheless he pointed out that the question appeared to him to be whether those evils did in fact arise out of the marriage law of Scotland; they did not appear to be traceable to the law itself or to the facilities for marriage but rather to the loose notions which the people themselves had of the ceremony,

Valerie and Michael Phillips, he is the manager of Gretna Hall Hotel, were married in what has become traditional Gretna style. Valerie said, 'I lived only a few miles away, but Michael comes from Wiltshire. He had been running hotels in Bournemouth and, fed up with the rat-race in the south, took a job with a Scottish chain of hotels. He came here in 1973. During that winter and early 1974 I joined a small photographic company. My work included taking photographs in the Smithy and the Hotel, and so I met Michael.

'Gretna Green did its bit – you can't escape romance here! We were married a year later. We went to the Register Office and then came to the Blacksmith's Shop, held hands over the anvil and repeated our vows.'

and to their own moral character. If they went to any part of Scotland, they would find that the people held such a marriage to be a legal and valid contract and as binding and indissoluble as any contract.

'Such marriages were performed throughout the length and breadth of the land and yet,' he asked, 'where is the country upon the face of the earth where the marriage contract was considered by the people more binding than that of Scotland?' In the very place where the marriage law existed in its fullest force they did not find these evils existing. He said that if they touched the law they would raise the Scottish people against them and it was well known that the Scottish people were not desirous of any interference. He felt that the evils arose not so much out of the facilities for marriage afforded by the law of Scotland as from the restrictiveness of the law in England. No one south of the border seemed willing even to consider that point.

Mr Mounsey replied, 'We have no wish to interfere with Scottish rights or the Scottish law in any way. All we want is to prevent the mischievous results of that law upon our own side of the border. The evils have been so great it is high time that some remedial measure is introduced.' He also told a story of a couple who were married after the Gretna fashion. She and her husband went away but soon after 'rued the day'. They agreed to go back to the 'priest' who had married them and when they did so, they told him they wished him to unmarry them. Unable to resist a double fee he took their money, muttered something mysterious over them, tore up the certificate and then turned one out of the front door and the other out of the back and they thought they were free. This caused much laughter at the meeting.

Mr Mounsey continued that he had spoken to the keeper of the Sark Tollbar and asked him, 'Is it possible that you did this thing?'

He said, 'I don't recollect the people, but I dare say we did.'

Mr Mounsey enquired if he was in the habit of doing this and the man admitted that he was, so the couple evidently believed they were as much unmarried as they had been married before. 'Are we to sit still and see such things going on before our very eyes and when we attempt to alter them, be told that the law of Scotland is being infringed?' he demanded.

The Rev R H Howard declared that he, as vicar of one of the largest parishes in Carlisle, had nearly 3,000 souls under his charge yet in the course of the last three years he had had 191 baptisms, 149 burials but only fourteen marriages. He quoted these figures to show how far persons availed themselves of the facilities the border marriages offered them. He did not pretend to explain the motive, because the expense of a journey to Gretna and the marriage fee they would have to pay when they got there, was far greater than the fee they would pay at the parish church or by going to the registrar. He could only conclude that they went there to avoid the publicity of the banns and in his opinion that was a most important consideration that ought not to be done away with.

The debate lasted for an hour and a half, at the end of which it was unanimously voted that the petition should be sent to Parliament to support Lord Brougham's bill. The new act was passed and came into force on 1 January, 1857. Its most important clause, as far as Gretna was concerned, was that one or both of the parties must have been born in Scotland, or must be domiciled in Scotland, or have resided there for three weeks before the date of marriage.

The Act was carefully designed to leave the Scots to their own time-honoured form of marriage, but to inhibit those who flitted over the border. On the day before it became law, John Murray at the Sark Tollbar married no less than sixty-one couples, and all the other 'priests' also had a heyday. Those who had fought for an alteration in the law breathed a sigh of relief. The inhabitants of Gretna thought that their village would soon lapse into the same obscurity as every other quiet place on the border. For about forty years it seemed to be just so – but then once again the village began to be caught in the tangled webs of young lovers.

The marriage trade at Gretna was never completely halted, but it lay more or less dormant. A few marriages took place from time to time. There was always some 'priest' who knew how to 'tie the knot' and, for some reason, at the beginning of this century, the demand for quick and quiet weddings again increased, perhaps it was the Boer War? At about the same time, the tourist trade sprang into being. Some railway official decided to run an excursion trip through the lake district, from Blackpool to Gretna.

One English couple who both work in Rome, and wanted to be married in Gretna, flew home from Italy, just for a few days. The bride's parents owned a small hotel at the edge of the Lake District, and unknown to her, her father hired a white Rolls Royce and arranged for all her family to gather for the wedding. Her sister rushed up from Guernsey and other relatives from Wales.

The passengers knew that hundreds of eloping couples had been married in the village, and they roamed around expecting to see some specific venue that could be linked to those romances; they became quite certain that the place they sought was the Smithy. Local people told them that the blacksmith had never performed any marriages but the tourists thought the Gretna folk were just being obstructive, spoiling their day out. They simply refused to believe that the Smithy had not been the principal setting for the marriages, and they gathered around it and peered through its windows, to the considerable annoyance of the smith and his wife.

With so much demand perhaps it was inevitable that in the end the sightseers should get what they wished for. In 1895, the Smithy had been bought as part of Gretna House estate by a farmer, Hugh Mackie. He decided that the visitors should be given what they were seeking, so he collected together some artefacts and in 1907, set up the old Smithy as a museum to runaway marriages. Tourists were fascinated. They came in ever increasing numbers and gazed at the souvenirs. The anvil became the centrepiece, and associated with it, was all the other paraphernalia of the forge and a growing collection of paintings, photographs, lithographs, newspaper cuttings and furniture.

From time to time couples still came to Gretna to be married, and as in the old days, these weddings usually took place at the inns or at the Sark Tollbar. On one occasion, however, a group of local young men were lounging about at the Smithy when a couple walked in and asked where they could get married. One of the lads was about to direct them to the Queen's Head Inn but another young man stopped him.

'Why not do it here?' he said. 'Run and fetch Hugh Mackie, and tell him to bring a "priest".' As one of the boys was about to set off he added, 'Tell him it should be good for a bottle of whisky.'

Hugh Mackie came, followed by the 'priest' and so the first of the next era of weddings was carried out at the old Smithy. Whether the lads ever got their bottle of whisky is a matter for debate, but they certainly deserved it. A new trend in marriages began. There were not too many at first, but enough to boost the reputation of Gretna once more and set it firmly on the tourist map, with its popularity ever increasing.

The three weeks residential qualification was something of a deterrent to young runaways but the 'priests' discovered that they personally could be legally covered by having a note printed at the bottom of the certificate. This stated: 'Unless either or both of the parties are natives of Scotland, the required 21 days Scottish residence immediately prior to the ceremony must be substantiated. On the signed declaration to that effect, the Scottish address is given as inscribed.' Any dispute that arose as a result of a false declaration fell on the heads of those who made it, and not on the 'priest' who accepted it without much questioning.

The First World War brought another change to the area. The Government decided that it was an entirely suitable place to build a cordite factory, between Gretna Green and the shore of the Solway. Until then only one or two farms or cottages stood in that remote area. The munitions factory meant that accommodation also had to be built for the workers and a whole new township sprang up almost overnight. There were houses and hostels, a staff club and a barracks, as well as the rather grim building of the factory itself. The work was so important to the war effort that in 1917 King George V and Queen Mary paid a visit to the factory and while they were there they could not resist taking a look at the renowned Blacksmith's Shop. It has been handed down that King George was highly amused by it, and that Queen Mary was by no means as strait-laced as photographs of her would suggest.

# CHAPTER TEN

# The Last of
# the Anvil Brides

One lady who remembers vividly being married at the Old Smithy was Mrs Jean Sturrock. 'It was on 27 June 1929. We weren't young, we weren't runaways, we weren't pursued, we were in our right minds,' she laughed at the memory. 'We were on holiday and we just walked into the Smithy and asked if we could get married.'

Jean Duff, as she was then, had been introduced to Harry Sturrock at a friend's house in Shields. She was nineteen and he was twenty-seven when they first started going out together; in those days it was usually on his motorbike. Jean worked as a fever nurse and never knew until she went in to work in the morning whether she would have any time off, but she used to send a message to Harry to let him know if she would be free. Then he would come and pick her up on his motorbike. 'You didn't need a helmet in those days,' Jean said, describing how she would hop up on the pillion and ride side-saddle in what she felt was a becomingly feminine manner.

After some time they became engaged, but though they often talked of marriage, Harry was such a shy man he just could not bear the thought of getting married in church with everyone looking at him. Jean was equally sure that she did not want to be married at a Register Office. Once Harry even suggested that they should get Jean's brother, who was a ship's captain, to take them three miles out to sea and marry them there.

Then, fifteen months after they had become engaged, they went on holiday. 'It was race-week Thursday,' Jean recalled. 'We'd been out Redcross way on the Wednesday and on the Thursday we went on this trip to Gretna. I remember it was beautiful weather and on the way Harry suggested we should get married in the Smithy and I aided and abetted. It was late when we rode through Carlisle and all the shops were closed so we could not buy a wedding-ring. Then we came to

101

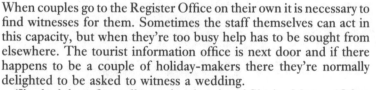

When couples go to the Register Office on their own it is necessary to find witnesses for them. Sometimes the staff themselves can act in this capacity, but when they're too busy help has to be sought from elsewhere. The tourist information office is next door and if there happens to be a couple of holiday-makers there they're normally delighted to be asked to witness a wedding.

'I've had them from all over the place,' said Shirley Moore. 'Often they're in holiday clothes, shorts and tee shirts. The important thing is that they must be over sixteen and they must understand English. Yesterday I rang up the tourist office and they told me an Australian couple had just left.

'I flew to the door and called to them just as they were getting into their car. The woman looked panic stricken. I said, "Would you mind witnessing a wedding for me," and they were both delighted to do that. It was only afterwards that the woman told me, "When you called out I thought we'd parked illegally, taken someone's space or something."

'The couple for whom they had acted as witnesses owned a guest house in Southport, and as the Australians were touring, and working their way down to London, they were invited to spend a night with the newlyweds, as their guests.'

Gretna. It was really countrified then, not like it is today. There was just this little white-washed cottage and we walked in and asked if we could get married. It was seven o'clock in the evening. I was wearing a grey flannel coat and a grey hat – we always wore hats in those days.

'Mr Rennison asked our ages. I was then twenty-three and Harry thirty-one. He asked if we lived in Scotland and we told him we came of Scots descent – Duff and Sturrock are both Scots names. My parents came from Peebles in Midlothian and Harry's father from Dundee, so although we lived in Newcastle, Mr Rennison put Midlothian down for the address. Then he went through the ceremony and clanged his hammer down on the anvil, and said to Harry – "Now you may kiss your bride."

'I was married with my engagement ring. There were some visitors in the Smithy and they acted as witnesses for us. Mr Rennison suggested we should have the wedding registered in Dumfries and we went to this office but of course it was closed, so we didn't bother any more.'

Off they went again on the motorbike, with the new Mrs Sturrock in her grey flannel coat and hat, riding side-saddle as usual. 'When we stopped that night I remember I was a bit embarrassed because I'd only got my engagement ring, and I twisted a bit of wool round it to hide the stones, and turned it round the other way, so the plain side was on top of my finger. We stayed in a little country place. I've forgotten exactly where, but to me, looking back on it, that day was full of romance.

'Next afternoon we called on some relatives of mine, and when we got there they wouldn't hear of us moving on any further that night. We were both too shy to tell them that we'd just been married – so I shared a box-bed with my cousin and my husband slept elsewhere.'

The following day they went home and broke the news to Jean's mother, who was not at all pleased with her. 'You'd no need to do a thing like that,' she said. 'What will the neighbours think?'

Jean didn't care what the neighbours thought. They had no home, but they had some furniture which they had been getting together since they had become engaged, and before long they found a small place to rent. Although the wedding was not registered this irregularity never presented any problems. When the time came for Harry to retire from work and claim the pension, they sent off the Gretna Green certificate, on its pale blue paper with the picture of the Smithy printed on top and Mr Rennison's signature below. It was accepted with no trouble at all. They were happily married for forty-nine years. Harry died a few months before they would have celebrated their golden wedding.

On one occasion they went back to Gretna on a coach trip. The driver called out as the coach stopped, 'This is Gretna Green, anyone want to get married? Anyone want to get divorced?' Jean and Harry looked at each other, but they were too self-conscious to say, 'We were married here.' Then, as they went round the museum, somehow their secret slipped out. At once there was a buzz of excitement as visitors insisted they must kiss again over the anvil and everyone wanted to take photographs of them, and they were asked to sign autographs. 'I felt like a VIP', Jean laughed.

Another couple who went to Gretna on a motorbike were Hilda Learmond and George Armitage. They intended to keep their wedding secret for two years but it didn't work out that way.

'George and I met in the Congregational Church at Innerleithen, Peebleshire,' Hilda said. 'He was church organist and I was in the choir. He used to wink at me in the mirror and, being only fifteen, I was covered in confusion. But before long we got together and then became constant companions. I was the eldest of eleven children and there were plenty of chores to be done, which didn't leave me much time for boyfriends, but somehow we managed. We spent many happy evenings at home, which usually ended with a sing-song around the organ. Mum

An elderly couple from Annan, great-grandparents now, have a laugh when they tell their story, which has lost nothing over the years. 'We intended to go to the cinema one evening but when we got there, the queue was so long we couldnae be bothered to wait. So we said let's go up to the hall and get Mr MacIntosh to marry us.' They did just that and were married there and then, over the anvil and went home to tell everybody.

They've now been married for forty-eight years. They're friends of Jim Jackson and when he got the job as guide at the Blacksmith's Shop, the old couple went to see the place again. Jim lifted the register out of the case, looked through it and found the entry of their marriage. The lady looked with tear-dimmed eyes at their young signatures, but her husband walked over to the anvil and kicked it. 'I assure you he was joking,' declared Jim. 'Because he worships her.'

and Dad were accomplished singers and George a professional musician, so it really was enjoyable.

'When I did go out with George, I had to be in by ten o'clock, and Dad would be looking out for me, dead on time, and no quarter given. George and I kept company for five years, and by then we were thinking seriously about marriage, but my parents would not hear of it. They refused even to discuss the subject – mainly because of lack of funds – so George and I decided we would go to Gretna Green.

'We started saving very hard and ten weeks later managed to have £2 each, and then we felt we were ready. I had arranged to spend a holiday with my aunt in Glasgow and travelled there by train, accompanied by my Granny and Grandad. George set off on his motorbike, and was supposed to be spending his holiday in Oban. Our arrangements worked out well, and we met up in Glasgow on the Saturday, just as we had planned. A crowd of us (I had several cousins) went to the pictures. Fred McMurray was the star. It makes me smile to think about it. I hadn't seen him before, and I thought he was just super, and I began to wonder if I was doing the right thing in arranging to marry George! But by the following morning, I'd forgotten all about Fred McMurray and knew that George was still the one for me, so on Monday morning we set off for Gretna on the motorbike without telling anyone.

'We arrived about twelve o'clock and really got cold feet. We sat outside on the seat for half an hour, wondering if we really should. I was still a bit scared when George at last persuaded me to go inside. Mr

Rennison seemed to notice us straight away and he asked – "Do you wish to get married?"

'"Yes," George said.

'Two witnesses were soon found and almost immediately we were clasping hands over the anvil and Mr Rennison began to go through the service. Before he had finished a bus load of people arrived. I didn't take much notice of them, they were strangers to me – but it turned out they were all from Peebles! And among them was a couple who knew my mother. The sightseers were thrilled to witness a real marriage.

'Clang! Mr Rennison hit the hammer on the anvil, and then I really knew it was too late to retract. It was 7 August 1933. I was twenty and George was twenty-two. The fee was one guinea.

'We then went to Dumfries and had bacon and eggs, and that was the first time I had ever eaten a meal in a restaurant. It cost 2s 6d. We had a photograph taken and that was another 5s. Then it began to rain, so we left for Glasgow. We called in to see a lady I knew who lent me a raincoat, as I was getting soaked on the pillion of the motorbike. The roads were very slippery and the motorbike had a bald tyre, and when we got to Buchanan Street in Glasgow we fell off three times. My biggest worry was that if I got killed, my parents would find out what we'd done, because I had the wedding certificate down the neck of my dress.

'Eventually we arrived safely at my aunt's house in Westerton and everything was lovely, including the weather. Nobody paid much attention to George and me – for everyone else it had been just another day. My cousins and I slept in a tent in the garden, and George was on a couch indoors. We stayed a few days there and then went home via Edinburgh. There we went to see a rugby match, Wales versus Scotland, at Murrayfield. That day I put on my wedding ring – just for a few hours. It was the first time I'd worn it since we'd been married, and I felt as if the whole crowd of 70,000 people were looking at it!

'We headed back to Innerleithen and I went to my home and George went to his. At this stage nobody was any the wiser, so everything in the garden was lovely. But I just had to tell someone, so I woke my sister Betty, and told her.

' "I wouldn't like to be you when Dad finds out!" she commented, and went back to sleep.

'Our secret lasted for only two weeks. The wedding notice had been put into one of the Glasgow papers and a friend of my parents saw it. Dad was furious, but it was not so much because we had eloped, but because he said we were not properly married. He wouldn't allow us to set up home together until we'd been married again, so we had another ceremony at the Church Manse on 20 October, just to please our parents. But we have always considered the Gretna Green marriage was our real anniversary.

'We managed to find two rooms to rent and we worked hard. Our daughter was born in 1935 and in 1937 we emigrated to New Zealand.' Their son John was born in 1940.

A few years later Mr and Mrs Charles Morton were married at the Smithy. 'I never wanted to get married in church,' said Elizabeth Morton. 'I had been to Gretna Green two or three times, just sightseeing of course, when I was out with other boys. I suppose I was a bit of a flirt in my young days, and we sometimes drove down to Gretna in a foursome. I always thought I would like to get married there.'

Elizabeth Fisher, as she was then, lived in Glasgow and worked in her mother's grocery shop. 'I met Charles because he used to come into the shop. I had known him for about a year before we got married. I was then twenty-five and Charles twenty-three. My mother didn't want me to marry him, she preferred the boy I had been engaged to before I met him. Charlie's mother did not want him to marry me either.'

A few days before their wedding Charles wrote a long love letter to Elizabeth, which she still keeps. It has been read and re-read so many times that the first and last pages are now missing, but it reveals clearly how seriously they both took the wedding and the vows they were about to make. With philosophical soul-searching, Charles wrote of the great step ahead of them, of the depth of his love for her, and how he was counting the hours to when they should declare themselves man and wife, linking their futures forever. He was then, and has always remained, a sincere and practising Christian, he plays the organ regularly at Sunday services and is deeply involved in church affairs.

On the day of her wedding Elizabeth worked in the shop until it closed, and in those days that was not until 9 pm on Saturdays. Then she rushed to her bedroom and quickly got changed into a white wedding dress borrowed from her sister-in-law and pinned a corsage of flowers to it. Her brother and his wife called for her in their car. They drove to the pre-arranged place, where Charles was ready and waiting and soon the four of them were on their way to Gretna Green.

'It was very, very romantic that night,' she recalled. 'The moon was shining, and when we got to Gretna the bells were just chiming midnight. The whole village was in darkness, and inside the Smithy there was just one electric light bulb shining. Mr Rennison was waiting for us – I had written to tell him we were coming. There was an elderly woman with him, I think she must have been his wife. There was this great black anvil, and we had to stand with our hands clasped over it.

'Mr Rennison went through the whole service from the prayer book. I think it took about half an hour. So we were actually married on Sunday morning, just after midnight, on 26 September 1937. Afterwards we drove back to Glasgow, to my brother's house. It must have been about

There are two assistant registrars at Gretna nowadays. Mrs Dorothy Taylor said, 'We still have quite a lot of people who phone up or even call in, and who think that Gretna is separate from the rest of Scotland, they believe, quite wrongly, that there are no preliminaries to be dealt with here. On Bank Holiday Monday, we had six couples who arrived here and wanted to be married straight away. One couple had driven overnight from London, and were quite exhausted. I was really sorry for them.'

three o'clock by then, and we made a cup of tea and then went to bed.

'On Sunday afternon we went back to my mother's house, and a lot of reporters turned up. How they had heard about it, I really don't know, unless Mr Rennison told them. Our photographs were plastered over all the papers. On Monday my mother held a sort of reception for us, just for our family, none of Charlie's would come. His mother said that we weren't properly married, and she would not have anything to do with us at all. So largely to please her, we had a religious service a fortnight later. It was at the church Charlie attended regularly, and the Minister wrote an endorsement on the back of the pale blue certificate with its picture of the Blacksmith's Shop, which had been given to us by Richard Rennison. The Minister wrote – "Married before me, according to the laws of the Church of Scotland, this day Oct 12th 1937."'

Elizabeth and Charles moved away from Scotland, and they have only been back to Gretna once since their wedding. They were on holiday, touring with a caravan, and they were surprised to find the Smithy so changed.

'It's quite different now, the anvil in a different place and organised as a curio shop instead of a wedding parlour. Oh, it was so romantic that night when we were there! I'd do the same again!'

Mr Rennison enjoyed his 'trade', he was always enthusiastic about marrying people. Agnes Law knew him as a friend of the family, because her mother lived in Gretna Green, close to the Smithy. When she was a young woman, Agnes moved to Coventry to find work, there she met Norman Lord and they began to go out together, usually in a foursome. Nine weeks later Agnes invited Norman home for the annual holiday.

'His mother and sister were moving house and he had nowhere to go,' Agnes said. 'And I was thinking that I'd get a free trip home on his motorbike.'

107

On the journey Norman suggested they should get engaged. Agnes was not too sure that she really wanted to, but he was persistent and then, assuming they would not get married for some time, she agreed. She reckoned without Mr Rennison. Soon after they arrived he called in to visit the family, and finding that Agnes had brought home a young man, gave him some thrifty Scottish advice.

'Don't waste your money on an engagement ring,' he said to Norman. 'I can marry you straight away.'

Agnes had been born in Scotland and therefore neither of them needed to reside there for the statutory twenty-one days. Norman took to the idea immediately, and first thing the next morning, at eight-thirty on the Wednesday to be precise, he proposed.

'No,' said Agnes. Having only just been talked into getting engaged, she had no wish to be married immediately.

Norman persisted throughout the day, continually asking her until finally, at about five o'clock, she gave in.

'Oh, all right.'

No sooner had she said it than he rushed her out to the motorbike and tore straight into Carlisle to buy a ring before the shops closed.

'Then I really felt I was committed,' Agnes said, 'and as soon as we got back, Norman arranged with Mr Rennison for the marriage to take place at eleven o'clock the next morning. While all this was going on, my mother was herself in Carlisle for the day and she knew nothing about the wedding arrangements until she came home at 10 pm.'

Mrs Law was absolutely staggered but since she had herself been married at Gretna, she quickly recovered. 'Well, Agnes – you're nineteen,' she said. 'I suppose you should know your own mind.'

Next morning Mrs Law sent telegrams all over the place notifying friends and relatives that Agnes was getting married at eleven o'clock that same day, and quite a number of people managed to get there.

'I'm sure most of them thought it must be a shot-gun wedding,' Agnes smiled. 'But it definitely wasn't. Our first child was born fourteen months later.'

Fortunately Mrs Law's house had several rooms, so the young couple managed not to see each other on the morning of the wedding, and when the appointed time came, Agnes walked across to the Smithy. She had only the suit she had worn to ride home on the motorbike, but with a fox fur and a cute little hat, she looked very smart. At the Smithy there was no sign of Norman. She was horrified, but he rushed in a few moments later, carrying a bunch of red roses. He had left the house earlier with her sister, Ernestine, and he wanted very much to get some flowers for Agnes. There was no florist in Gretna, so he walked along looking into gardens until he found one with some lovely red roses. He

Jim Jackson recalls one special couple, 'They were runaways. They left their families down south in England saying they were coming on holiday to Scotland. But they had a rather important pre-arranged appointment at Gretna Green. He was seventy-six years of age and she was seventy-four, a widower and a widow, and they told us that their families had encouraged them to get married, but they had decided to keep it secret, because they knew that there would have been so much fuss. So here in Gretna Green those runaway senior citizens had a quiet but joyful wedding, and after the civil ceremony they came here to the Blacksmith's Shop, and repeated their vows over the anvil. Then they sent holiday postcards to everyone back home saying we are no longer enjoying a holiday – but a honeymoon!'

knocked on the door and asked if he could buy some as he was getting married and wanted them for his bride. The lady refused to sell him any but she gave him some.

'Even at such short notice my mother, bless her, managed to give a reception and she provided everything except a cake. Her house, Hazeldean, was only a hundred yards or so from the Smithy. In recent years it has been turned into an hotel, but that was where we spent our first night. The second night after our marriage we stayed with my brother (who was killed in North Africa in the war) and his wife and children at Fulwood Barracks, Preston, on our way back to Coventry.

'It was a long trip back and that pillion seat was really hard. I was tired and sore and when we finally arrived the whole of Norman's family were waiting. They had moved that same week from Lancashire to Coventry and though Norman had written to tell them the news, they had never met me. It wasn't a happy reception – and who can blame them? It was such a shock for them. In fact things were so bad that Norman picked up our cases and said we'd go – but I managed to calm him down.

'Less than a month after our wedding, war was declared. Norman and I lived with his mother and sister until the Christmas, when at last we managed to get a house to rent. We had no furniture, pots, pans or anything to set up a home – on our return from Gretna we had only 2s 4d between us. But we worked hard and we managed.

'I had to wait twenty-five years for an engagement ring. Norman bought it for our Silver Wedding Anniversary, and we had our wedding cake then too.'

Now retired and living near Boston, in Lincolnshire, Norman and Agnes Lord can look back over fifty years of married life, and for every anniversary Norman has made sure that Agnes has a bunch of red roses – usually by growing them himself. They have a son and a daughter and three grandchildren.

'It hasn't been an easy life,' says Agnes. 'But love grows and I'm sure will continue to do so.'

CHAPTER ELEVEN

# The End of the
# Irregular 'Priests'

Lord Brougham's Bill was not completely ineffective. Nowadays the museum guides conducting mock marriages at the blacksmiths' shops refer to it as introducing a 'three week cooling off period'. This gets a laugh from the crowd but there is no evidence that it ever actually dampened the ardour of young lovers. What it did provide was a chance for parents to catch up with the runaways.

In the year 1929 an aircraft was used for the first time, this was in pursuit of a couple of seventeen-year-olds. The young man was the son of a wealthy Member of Parliament. Hearing that their son had eloped with his girlfriend, and was heading for Scotland, the MP and his wife rushed to Croydon Aerodrome and chartered an air taxi. 'At more than a hundred miles an hour,' reported the newspapers – 'the plane sped northwards, but overtaken by darkness, the pilot was unable to go further than Blackpool.' Meanwhile the young couple arrived in Gretna on the 7.15 am train from London and went to a boarding-house, where they had breakfast and tidied themselves up, ready for the ceremony. They walked into the Smithy soon after 9 am and asked Mr Rennison if he would marry them. It was obvious to him that they were runaways. 'They were just like two innocent children out for a holiday trip,' he told reporters afterwards. All he could do was to explain the law and point out that they would have to be resident in Scotland for twenty-one days before they could be legally married.

'I never saw a young couple more dismayed and disappointed,' Mr Rennison said. 'I couldn't forbear smiling at the dismay in their young faces.'

Knowing the young man's father was hot in pursuit, they dared not stay in Gretna, so they decided to carry on to Glasgow and left by the next train. Before they left the Smithy, they signed the visitor's book and the young man said ruefully, 'It's not Mr and Mrs – yet.'

The delay gave the parents time to contact the police who traced the pair to an hotel in Union Street where they had booked two rooms for the night. There followed a friendly talk together and finally all four left by train to return to London amid a throng of reporters and photographers. The lovers had won from the parents their consent to an engagement. Their plans had been thwarted but it was just this sort of dramatic chase that kept the name of Gretna almost continually on the front pages of the daily papers.

Richard Rennison was the best known of the 'priests' during this era. He started 'marrying the folk', as he called it, in 1927 and from then until the law was changed in 1940, he claimed to have conducted 5,147 marriages. He was dark haired, ruddy of complexion, a businessman. He enjoyed and was proud of his 'marrying-trade', and was often reported as making remarks such as 'It was a delight to marry such a charming couple.' If anyone asked him what hours he kept, he replied 'Doctor's Hours', carrying on the old tradition of Gretna 'priests' of being ready to answer a call at any hour of the day or night. He lived in the cottage that is now the souvenir shop for the Smithy, so he had only to walk through the door to the Marriage Room. On one occasion on New Year's Day in 1931 he returned from a funeral and found eight couples waiting on the doorstep wishing to be married.

Rennison came from the Borders, near Hexham, where he had worked as a saddler. By sheer good fortune he arrived at Gretna just when Hugh Mackie was looking for someone to take the position of resident 'priest' at the Smithy. Richard Rennison started almost straight away and he was said to have the right knack for it, being a talkative sort of fellow and a bit of a showman. He didn't dress particularly smartly, he just wore an ordinary suit, and was of average height and rather stout. It amused him and pleased him that if his name was spelt backwards, it read 'no sinner'.

Marriages began to flourish in Gretna once again, another boom was on the way. The Sark Tollbar also stepped up its business, carrying on the tradition from the old days. Arthur Stephenson was the last 'priest' there but in the mid-1930s the Tollbar was bought by Hugh Mackie who decided to set it up simply as a museum. Thereafter all the wedding-trade was directed to the Blacksmith's Shop at the Headlesscross.

Hugh Mackie's monopoly was short-lived. In 1938, Gretna Hall was bought by David Ramsay Mackintosh, a local garage owner. Long before that time the Hall had reverted to being a private house. David Mackintosh decided not only to reopen it as an hotel, he was determined also to bring it back into the marriage business. Disregarding the historic fact that the old weddings had all taken place inside the hotel

Romance for Robert Peck and his teenage sweetheart Florence started nearly fifty years before their wedding. They had been parted when as a young soldier he was posted to the West Indies, because neither of them had been good letter writers. Each of them fell in love again and married someone else. Time passed and sadly they lost their respective spouses. Robert returned to England, left the army, and became a senior officer in the Manchester Fire Brigade.

After he retired he went to Weymouth on holiday, and there, quite by chance, he met Florence. Even after those decades spent apart, they both recognised each other instantly, and seemed to take up again where they had left off. They spent the rest of Robert's holiday together and a few weeks later he invited Florence to accompany him on a trip to Scotland. He didn't tell her that he was making arrangements with the registrar until they arrived at Gretna! Florence was astonished but she had no doubts about accepting his proposal, and they were married.

Robert and Florence revisit the village every year and call on Miss Bryden. During one of their visits they were asked to act as witnesses for a marriage. The couple were the headmaster of a primary school, aged thirty-six and his bride of sixteen – one of the stories that hit the national headlines because the man had been living with the girl's mother, before he ran away with her daughter.

Even adverse publicity never seems to damage Gretna's image for long and the following year the graph of weddings rose yet again. In the early 1980s there were more weddings in the summer than in the winter. Now it's just a steady stream all the year.

itself, Mackintosh converted the stables and coach-house into a 'Smithy'. He even went so far as to employ a real blacksmith to work there on occasions, but the real purpose of the new forge was to participate in the wedding and tourist trade.

David Mackintosh looked a typical Scot. He always wore a kilt and enjoyed his nickname of the 'kilted priest'. He was a big, bluff man, ruddy faced, very active and much more extrovert than Richard Rennison. His niece remembers him as generous, 'Always worth the price of a ticket to the cinema,' she said, with affection. She often worked at the Hall and was sometimes called upon to be a witness to a wedding. The pay was quite good, about half a crown (12½p) and the only qualification was that, like the bride and groom, witnesses had to be over sixteen.

Above the door of Gretna Hall, David Mackintosh set up a sign with the words 'The Original Marriage House'. This led to a court case, a battle of the signs, which was fought fiercely between the owners of the two blacksmith's shops. It was contested in a long drawn out hearing in Edinburgh; Hugh Mackie lost the case but David Mackintosh was awarded only derisory damages. The participants are both dead but some of the rivalry they stirred up remains to this day, though over the years they have learned to co-exist without bitterness. Each place has a rightful claim to its share of the history of elopements, and as the coachloads of sightseers pour in, there is obviously ample business for both.

In the two years left after 1938, during which anvil weddings were legally possible, a steady trade built up in the Smithy behind Gretna Hall. They had the advantage of being nearest to the railway station and the first of the smithies on the road from Carlisle. In that short time 430 weddings took place there.

There were always others who were willing to conduct weddings, usually in private houses. One of these was known as Granny Graham. Mrs Graham proudly proclaimed herself as the 'original priestess', but she was said to look 'just a typical granny, a smallish old body, dressed in black'. There was money to be made but everyone knew it could not last for much longer, especially when in 1935, Parliament set up a committee to look into the subject of irregular marriages in Scotland.

Many of the couples who married there in the 1920s and 1930s were more mature people, but there were always a great many who eloped to escape parental opposition in some form or other. Sometimes there were religious differences between the families, which in those days was a source of much more bitterness than is generally the case now. Often there was a general lack of money, which caused parents to try to persuade their sons and daughters to put off marrying until they had saved up enough to get a good and respectable start in life. With low wages and unemployment it could take years. A few extrovert couples actually courted the publicity of a Gretna wedding, which could be useful if they were trying to make a name for themselves on the stage or in films. They could be sure of getting their names in the papers if they arranged something a little bizarre, like being married by flashlight. Some rushed headlong to Gretna from the town where they were currently appearing in a show, and got back again without missing a performance. In one case, the couple were married 'standing upon gold' as one newspaper reported. For the general public, however, the most exciting elopements were when there was a difference in social class, with rich and angry parents in pursuit. Then the reporters from the national dailies and even from overseas, turned up in force and usually it

114

*left* 'Gretna Green or the Red-Hot Marriage. Oh! Mr Blacksmith ease our Vains – and Tie us fast in Wedlocks Chains.' (*The Leadenhall Press*)

*below left* Shades of the past. Eileen Gailey and Bishla Gorzynski were married in 1986.

*below right* Keith and Amanda Brunt from Belfast, 13 June 1988.

The Dutch giant, Jan Van Albert, 9 feet 3½ inches tall, visited the Blacksmith's Shop when he was thinking of marrying there. Mr Mackie, himself over 6 feet 3 inches, is on the right.

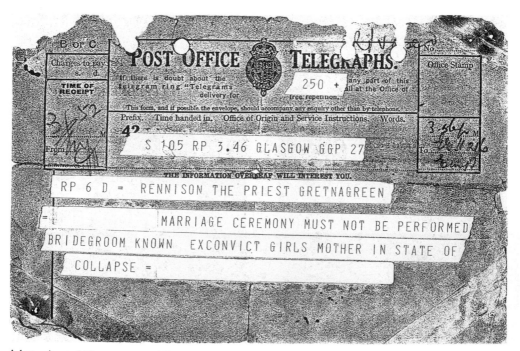

A last minute bid to stop a wedding in the early thirties. 'Marriage ceremony must not be performed. Bridegroom known ex-convict. Girl's mother in state of collapse.' (*Mr & Mrs Adair Houston*)

To His Highness the Lord or Count of the Village/County Gretna-Green!

with thankends in for kind ans humbl chris we save u King o]

LA POSTE
renseignements taxix téléphone
(1) 42.88.67.8

U.K. Angleterre

PARIS 77 (131)
6-1 1986
R.RENE
6-1-86

To His Excellence A.H. Lord or Count of Gretna Green (near Dumfries)

Scotland
Ecosse

Any strangely addressed envelope goes to the Register Office.

Just married over the anvil by Mr Rennison, Agnes and Norman Lord, August 1939. (*Mr & Mrs Norman Lord*)

James and Isabel Goldsmith, 9 Januar
1954. (*BBC Hulton Picture Library*)

Sir James Goldsmith at the wedding of h
daughter, Isabel, 1973. (*The Keystor
Collection*)

ave and Jan Cooper reaffirm their vows over
e anvil on their wedding day, 4 September
063. (*Mr & Mrs David Cooper*)

*ow left* Robert and Brenda Simpson, 1000th
ple to marry at Gretna Register Office.

*ow right* Americans Jeff Brown and Diane
lley were married in the Old Blacksmith's
op by Adam Barr.

PLATE IV.

A TRIP TO GRETNA GREEN.

THE RECONCILIATION.

London, Published by J. J. Marks.

9, Long Lane, Smithfield, May 1, 1817.

was the young couple whose plight captured the hearts and sympathy of the readers.

Richard Rennison was ever on the lookout for ways of boosting his business. On one occasion he sent a letter to one of the national newspapers, saying he knew of many lonely bachelors and spinsters who would like to get married. The response he received was even greater than he anticipated and proved his point. Some of these wistful letters are still displayed at the Old Blacksmith's Shop.

22.4.38

Dear Mr Rennison,
      Seeing in the Daily Express yesterday about 9 lonely men looking for brides so I thought I would write to you to see if you would find me a husband. I belong to the north, am 26 years old, quite good-looking, kind-hearted, sporty once I come to know folks ways and I am a domestic servant. I enclose latest photo. I have been in Edinburgh 4 years but was born in the country. So trusting I will be lucky in getting a reply –
p.s. Do not put it in the paper as my parents would be angry with me.

Dear Sir,
      I was very interested with your letter in the Dumfries Standard re: the young lady of twenty one years who feels herself lonely and wishes to correspond with a Gentleman in view of marriage as a matter of fact I feel lonely myself and would like to correspond with the lady referred to. I am in business in Dumfries and unmarried and I live with a Housekeeper and I feel I would like to settle down with this young lady. Of course I hope you will treat this as confidential and if the young lady is good enough to respond to this letter I shall be pleased to furnish her with all information required.

Dear Sir,
      In answer to your advert Thursday Daily Express for Brides – I am a lonely young woman with a daughter of 9 years and would like to meet a nice young man in comfortable circumstances I am a good housekeeper and can cook, knit and sew. I have kept house for my father for the past 14 years,
      Yours truly

Excursions to Gretna Green were so popular that a report in August 1929 stated 'the rush of would-be visitors from Morecambe to see the romantic village was so great that two trains had to be put on instead of one. They carried 1000 passengers, but even then more than 200 people were left behind. Two hours were allowed at Gretna Green for sight-seeing.' Similar excursions were run from Blackpool.

Every sensational headline was a boost for Gretna Green, weddings increased in number and the tourist trade expanded. People drove in by charabanc, steamed in by train, and pedalled along in great groups belonging to cyclist's touring clubs. They looked at the exhibits, bought souvenirs and sometimes just waited around hoping for that added excitement, the chance to witness a real runaway wedding.

The committee presided over by Lord Morison produced its report at the end of 1936. One of the main causes of concern was that so few irregular marriages were registered. This should have been done at the Sheriff's office within three months, but it meant an additional journey to Dumfries accompanied by the witnesses, so most couples simply did not bother. This sometimes presented legal difficulties in later life, particularly in the event of divorce. Yet, though it was supposed to be a requirement, lack of registration in no way invalidated the marriage.

Cases were also reported in which proper records were not kept. Informal weddings still took place in various parts of Scotland, in the old way, by a simple declaration before two witnesses. The Gretna 'priests' kept their records with pride and care, so this often did not apply to them but they were condemned for slackness over the twenty-one days residential qualification. A false declaration on this point could nullify the marriage. 'Claverhouse' quotes a case in 1919, as an example, when the parents of a young English lady refused their consent to her union with an American, on the grounds that she was too young. The couple resolved to elope and marry in Edinburgh. Then faced with the need to stay in Scotland for twenty-one days, the bridegroom persuaded two witnesses to make a false declaration of residence.

'After the marriage they returned to England and booked a passage on the liner *Olympic*, enjoying a short honeymoon until the vessel was due to sail. Two hours before the *Olympic* was to leave Southampton, two detectives crossed her gangway with a warrant for arrest. The young people were taken to Edinburgh and the bridegroom was tried for suborning two witnesses to make a false statement before the Sheriff. He was sentenced to two months imprisonment. Their ignorance of the Scots law and the evident high character of the couple aroused public sympathy; an American family befriended the bride, and a leading parish minister arranged that a marriage in legal form should be celebrated at the earliest possible moment. Church law required only fifteen days residence in Scotland, and a further wait of forty-eight hours before the wedding.

'All this was arranged, and the Prison commissioners consented to the

Mrs Shirley Moore, an assistant registrar, said, 'They say romance is dead, but there's no sign of it here. People say to me – "Weddings, weddings every day, five days a week – don't you get sick of them?" But you know every wedding's different, every couple is different.

'Quite a lot of the people we marry come back here on their anniversary – they wouldn't do that to just any Register Office, it's the special thing about Gretna. Some come back from many years ago and ask if they may see the register.'

bridegroom going to church to be married. The ceremony was completed, the registration forms duly signed in the vestry, when the Governor of Calton Gaol made a dramatic appearance, drew a document from his pocket and announced that the Secretary for Scotland had consented to the immediate release of the bridegroom and of the two witnesses. The poor bride collapsed but soon recovered. There were general congratulations and rejoicing. The young couple prepared to leave for New York, but before leaving the ex-prisoner said he had been most fairly and courteously treated throughout.'

A new Marriages (Scotland) Act was formulated and debated at length in Parliament. One speaker quoted a couple who went to the Dumfries Sheriff's Clerk to register their marriage in the correct manner, but they ran into difficulties because neither could speak English. In fact, both were from Finland. The Sheriff then questioned the 'priest' as to how he could conduct a proper marriage for such people. The 'priest' had a ready explanation. When the couple arrived, they did not have the proper qualification, he said, but they resided in Scotland for twenty-one days and by that time they could speak the language and had learned the words of the ceremony. He added that there was an interpreter present at the time.

Referring to the laxity of the ruling on residential qualification, Mr Barr, MP for Coatbridge, Lanarkshire, said: 'Within my knowledge a Member of Parliament was married at Gretna Green and I took the trouble to go into the library of the House, where I found he had made twenty-six Divisions during the twenty-one days he was supposed to be resident in Scotland. Those of us who represent Scotland are in the habit of being a good deal in Scotland, and a good deal here, but we have not yet attained what was attained in that case, the power of making numerous Divisions in this house, and yet being in continuous residence in Scotland.'

117

As in previous years Scottish members were reluctant to have the law of their land changed. One member, Mr Mathers said, 'In Scotland we are generous in our consideration of human frailties.' Mr Gibson pointed out, 'Throughout history the law of Scotland has dealt with marriage more kindly than it has in England. This Bill seems to be an attempt to bring our Scottish law down to the lower level of law in England.' He feared it would result in more illegitimate children and enable men to seduce young women with promises of marriage and more easily shrug off their responsibilities thereafter.

The debate made no bones that the chief purpose for which the Morison Committee was set up was to stop the marriages at Gretna, which were seen to be 'Just about the last word in commercialised robbery in Scotland.' Nevertheless it was admitted that marriages there were cheaper than those before the Sheriff, where the cost was reckoned to be at least two guineas (£2 10p). That was considered far too expensive for most people, so arrangements were made to set up Register Offices throughout Scotland. It was decided that one of these should be at Gretna.

Anywhere in the world where marriages can be performed quickly and easily becomes known as the Gretna Green of that country. The United States has its counterpart in a small town called Elkton, Maryland, which lies just south of the State border with Pennsylvania and within easy reach of New Jersey, Delaware and New York.

Just as the change in the marriage law of England sent runaways hastening to Gretna after 1754, it was the 1913 amendments to the marriage laws of neighbouring states that brought thwarted lovers pouring into Elkton. In both places there were people only too eager to cash in on the 'trade' – and often they were not too scrupulous about doing so. Many bizarre characters sprang into prominence in Elkton, and the names of famous people are among those who chose to marry there.

In Maryland, prior to 1938, it was possible for a marriage to take place in as little as two minutes. Girls could marry at twelve and boys at fourteen provided they had parents' consent. Otherwise it was eighteen for the bride and twenty-one for the groom but there were special concessions available if the girl was pregnant. The ease with which marriages could be arranged brought couples into the State in their hundreds, and since Elkton was the first town most of them came to, there they stepped off the train.

Very soon marriages became big business. The law stipulated that the religious service had to be conducted by a Minister but that was no problem. Judge James F Evans of Cecil County Circuit Court decreed,

Derek and Janet Kenyon have returned to Gretna for their anniversary every year since their marriage in April 1982, and now they would feel something was missing in their lives if they didn't manage to get there. It is not easy, they live on the border of Norfolk and Suffolk where Derek is a screen-printer, and Janet a music teacher, in fact they are both talented musicians and they often have engagements to be fulfilled.

In their 'spare time' they are converting their home from a near derelict condition. But every April they manage to get away for the four or five days necessary to make the trip and meet again the friends they made when they were there for their wedding. They stay at the same hotel and book the same room, they even stop at the same Little Chef, and Derek orders the same meal. The piper at the Old Blacksmith's Shop always remembers when they are due and looks out for them, ready to play his pipes specially for them.

'Most people go out for a nice dinner for their anniversary,' said Janet. 'We do that too, only we travel three hundred miles for it!'

'If a group of people get together and appoint a man their preacher, he is qualified to marry. The group may live in another state and disband right afterwards, but the preacher remains in good standing unless he is unfrocked.'

One of the first to exploit the situation was the Reverend William R Moon, a sixty-year-old Baptist minister, who came from the Far West. He was a tall, impressive-looking man, with a sonorous voice. He moved into Elkton, set up shop on East Main Street, and erected a sign designating himself as the 'Only Original Marrying Parson'. Other matrimonial entrepreneurs also moved in, and soon a plethora of advertising signs began to shriek their messages.

One priest, the Reverend Edward C Minor from Baltimore put up about fifty signs in and around Elkton. He advertised his services so successfully, even paying scouts to bring couples in, that in nine years he performed 17,863 marriages. He was so offensively brash that eventually he was unfrocked but that did not drive him out of business. He hired a young preacher from West Virginia's Free Will Baptist Church, the Reverend Percy K Lambert, to act as his assistant and perform the actual ceremonies for him.

After a time the Reverend Lambert set up on his own, advertising his marriage shop with electric lights, THE WEDDING BELL FOR

MARRIAGE CEREMONIES. SERVICES AT ALL HOURS. He had thousands of handbills distributed, offering 'nonsectarian wedding services for Catholics and Hebrews, which are accepted by their churches at face value'. Since it was illegal to charge for the wedding, he listed his expenses: rent, phone, secretary, legal fees etc; and for these estimated his fee at $10.

Many other parsons moved in and their signs and slogans festooned the town, to the disgust and dismay of most of the residents. Competition was fierce as close on 200 couples arrived every week. One trio of ministers set up a 'marriage-mill' to provide a round-the-clock service, working a rota of day and night shifts. Elkton's marrying parsons had no congregations, nor did they perform any other pastoral functions. The established churches in the town – Catholic, Episcopal, Presbyterian, Baptist and a number of independent sects all had their own ministers. They would marry a couple when requested to do so, in the normal round of their duties, but they played no part in the quickie 'marriage trade'.

Sensational stories in the newspapers provided continual publicity as headlines declared: 'Heiress elopes to Elkton'; 'Marrying parson seals 1,000th couple'; 'Child-bride marries in Maryland'. Sometimes the stories were linked to famous people: film actress Joan Fontaine; Babe Ruth, the baseball player; and John Mitchell, former Attorney General. Other well-known names include Billie Holliday, the tennis professional Fred Perry and golfer Dorothy Hurd.

Couples arriving at the railroad station were met by a small fleet of taxi-drivers. 'Pop' Cann was in on the business from its beginning, literally back in horse and buggy days. He was astute enough to organise a syndicate with which he managed to corner the parking franchise from the Pennsylvanian Railroad Company, so that almost all arrivals were carried in his cabs, and taken to the parsons with whom he had agreements. Two parsons were actually on the payroll of the syndicate at $50 a week.

In the 1930s, there were reports of disgraceful behaviour when rival touts clamoured and fought for custom. They were said to 'swarm all over' any likely looking couple, shouting and gesticulating. It was no wonder that many townspeople were so concerned at such scenes that they pleaded for the marriage laws of Maryland to be amended. This eventually came about in 1938, when a forty-eight hour wait was imposed between the issue of the licence and the legalising of the marriage.

The unscrupulous operators of the 'marriage-mill' sought for ways of evading these restrictions, but the law was enforced by heavy fines and imprisonment. It was further strengthened in 1944 when it became illegal to solicit either by word or advertisement. A writer in the 1950s stressed the disappointment of couples who found they had to wait two days to wed and remarked on the hardship they experienced, as they 'stuck it out' almost penniless, evading all attempts by furious parents to dissuade them. It seems little compared with the three weeks at Gretna.

The final curb on the exploitation of those who wished to marry in Elkton was procured in 1964, with the abolition of the legislation which required a 'religious' ceremony. Yet, thousands of couples have been married there since then. Some couples now choose to marry in Elkton to follow a family tradition, because their parents or grandparents were married there, especially when they have 'lived happily ever after'.

At the Cecil County Courthouse, which covers the town, they do nothing but issue marriage licences, and perform civil marriage ceremonies. In 1982 they issued 5,500 wedding licences, mostly to people living outside the area. The walls of the marriage bureau, where civil marriages are carried out, are lined from floor to ceiling with thick white binders, each of which holds 500 marriage licences. That number could well be issued in a single month.

Only one of the former marriage houses remains, known as The Little Wedding Chapel. It is but one small room in an early nineteenth century house on Main Street, situated conveniently opposite to the Cecil County Courthouse. Business is pretty good there, too. The Chapel's services are available to any couple who have obtained a valid marriage licence, and a minister is always available. Some couples dress for the occasion in full regalia, long gown and veil for the bride, a 'tuxedo' for the groom. Others turn up in jeans or dungarees and sweatshirt. Most just wear normal everyday fashion.

Just as in Gretna, Valentine's Day is one of the most popular dates to choose for weddings. In 1980, there were forty-two weddings at the chapel on that one day. Other favourite times are during the month of June, a traditional wedding month and, on a more mundane level, during Christmas week – to take advantage of tax concessions in the new year. Weddings seldom take place on a Friday 13th.

Elkton's history of marriages goes back less than eighty years, but its reputation lives on and the fifty years of its heyday has given it a lasting fascination, linking for ever with the romance of runaway marriages.

# CHAPTER TWELVE

# Isabel Patino and Jimmy Goldsmith

In 1953, two days before the Coronation of Her Majesty Queen Elizabeth, Isabel Patino, one of the richest heiresses in the world, celebrated her eighteenth birthday and her father gave a lavish party at Claridges in London. It was there that James Goldsmith was first introduced to her and the rapport between them was instantaneous. He was twenty years old, tall, good-looking and his ready wit made her laugh and feel happy. The spark that was kindled in Isabel that evening led to the elopement which was to hit the headlines of the world's Press six months later – and start the rush to Gretna all over again.

Isabel, beautiful, dark-haired and gifted with youthful, unsophisticated charm, was the daughter of the fabulously rich Don Antenor Patino. It had been her grandfather, Simon Patino, who had amassed the family's vast fortune when by some lucky chance, he stumbled across an abandoned tin mine high in the remote Andes mountains in Bolivia. Simon Patino was at that time a humble South American greengrocer but he was astute enough to recognise the potential of his find. With determination and hard work he managed to re-open the mine, although at that time he could never have calculated the enormous wealth it would produce. Within a few years, Simon Patino was richer than the Bolivian Government itself, and in 1925 he had an estimated income of £100,000 a day. He took full advantage of his money to increase and consolidate his wealth. He became the Bolivian ambassador to France and built a magnificent legation in Paris. He also built palatial houses in Biarritz and Nice, as well as three mansions in Bolivia, whose cost alone was ten million pounds, and he never even visited two of them.

Isabel's father, Don Antenor, was married to a Bourbon princess, a niece of King Alfonso of Spain. Simon had developed a passionate interest in royalty and felt that only the most aristocratic of beings could be a fit match for his millions. His daughter was also married to a

Spanish grandee, a Marquis of such exalted birth that he was allowed to keep his hat on in the presence of the king. Isabel was born in Paris in 1935 and was the younger of two lovely daughters of a loveless match. She grew up in the midst of luxury. After the German invasion of France in 1940, the Patinos fled from war torn Europe via Spain, and sailed to New York where they took a suite at the Hotel Plaza, where Christina and Isabel attended school at the Convent of the Sacred Heart. Their grandfather, Simon, died in 1947.

In 1951, when Isabel was sixteen, Don Antenor decided life in Europe had sufficiently recovered from the war for him to take his family back to Paris. There Isabel continued her education, being chauffeur driven every morning to a finishing school in Versailles and fetched back in the afternoon. She led an almost cloistered life, and was never allowed out except in the company of her parents or with her chaperone, Mlle de Vassal, who was also a friend of the family.

Christina and Isabel, nurtured and raised with the best of everything that money could buy, grew up into beautiful young ladies. They were well educated, charming and talented – Isabel could speak six languages fluently. They were also girls of spirit, and not always meekly obedient to their overbearing father. Each of them had a chaperone, a chauffeur and a secretary, whose duties included watching over their every movement. Staff in all the Patino households had to make out a report every night on the exact whereabouts from minute to minute of the two girls.

Once Christina made a bid for freedom and she ran off with an American from Madrid. But the Patino procedures for preventing this sort of thing had been well planned and in a very short time the rebellious daughter was found and brought home. Shortly after that another suitor came seeking her hand. He was, at that time, a working director of a travel agency from which he drew a modest salary, but his name was Prince Marc de Beauvau-Craon. He was twenty-nine years old, and was the sole surviving member of one of the oldest families in France. He owned an ancient and beautiful castle, the Château d'Haroue near Nancy, which he visited for occasional weekends. It was reported that when Prince Marc asked for the hand of Christina, Don Antenor Patino looked him up in the French equivalent of *Debrett*, then said, 'You can marry Christina.' It was the wedding of the year in Paris.

The following spring the whole world was looking towards London. The coronation of HM Queen Elizabeth was approaching and Don Antenor decided to take Isabel to London. It was an exciting time to visit, she had never been there before and was delighted with everything. The Capital was thronging with people of all nationalities, and there was a heady excitement in the air. For Isabel Patino, after her birthday party, that excitement was heightened by the charming attentions of Jimmy Goldsmith.

By most standards he was a rich young man. His father was chairman of a company that owned a string of hotels and was a director of the Savoy Group in London. Young as he was, Jimmy was a director of seven French companies. He had left the British army only a few months earlier, in April 1953, and almost immediately he started his own small business, which he acquired for £200. Isabel met him several times at parties during her two week visit to London and she was as eager as he for their meetings to continue after she returned to the marble palace at Plassy, even though she knew her father disapproved.

In France she had to give her chaperone the slip to meet Jimmy alone but it was not too difficult. She invented excuses to visit girlfriends at their houses, but after the chauffeur dropped her off, she would take a taxi to her rendezvous with Jimmy. Her father had given her a beautiful leopardskin coat, an eye-catching garment, as a birthday present and many people noticed the lovely girl walking hand in hand through streets of Paris with the tall, blond Englishman. Before long this indiscretion was reported to Don Antenor.

Being eighteen gave Isabel no legal freedom, she had to wait until she was twenty-one before she could direct her own life. Her father gave her strict instructions that she was never to meet Jimmy alone again, though he did concede that she could see him at parties, or in the presence of her chaperone. He also sent for Jimmy Goldsmith and advised him that he did not consider him in any way a fitting match for Isabel; there was little the young man could offer in comparison to the Patinos. He was an old Etonian but there was no blue blood in his veins, and Don Antenor had about half a dozen royal bachelors in mind, who might make suitable husbands for his daughter.

To emphasise his point still further, he added, 'You must understand, we come from a very old Catholic family.'

'That's perfect!' agreed Jimmy. 'I come from a very old Jewish family.'

Despite this opposition, Jimmy and Isabel continued to meet,

It has been known for a whole bus load to arrive for a wedding. That was the arrangement made to suit both families when one was from England and the other from Scotland, and Gretna was more or less half-way between them. That bride had twelve bridesmaids and a page-boy, and the bus driver put down a red carpet from the bus door to the Register Office.

although it was much more difficult. Princess Windisch-Gretz was engaged to watch over Isabel and she did so with rigid vigilance. Whenever she went to parties, shopping, to the races, visiting friends or anywhere else, her chaperone went too. The Princess accompanied Isabel when she was a guest at the wedding of Jimmy's brother Edward to Jill Pretty, a Dior mannequin. Somehow or other the young couple managed to see each other quite frequently and it became increasingly evident that they were deeply in love. Isabel's parents grew more and more alarmed. They were by no means a united couple but they were in complete accord on this issue. As far as they were concerned it was absolutely out of the question for their daughter to marry Jimmy Goldsmith.

Occasionally, Isabel managed to give her chaperone the slip, so that she and Jimmy could meet alone. They both realised that their only hope of happiness together would be to elope and so they began to make plans. Jimmy instructed a London solicitor to look into the requirements of a marriage in Scotland. Runaway marriages to Gretna had been few and far between since the change in the law had put an end to the simple marriage by declaration, north of the border. Mr Smith's investigations enabled him to assure Jimmy and Isabel that, since they were over sixteen, they could be married at any Register Office in Scotland without parental consent. The only essential provision was that they must have proof of their fifteen days residential qualification and then give seven days public notice, which excluded Sundays. The three weeks 'cooling-off' period.

It all seemed unbelievably simple. Then, almost as if he had guessed of their scheme, Don Antenor suddenly sent Isabel to Casablanca for a month's holiday. She was hurried away without even a chance to let Jimmy know where she was going. It took him two days to discover where she was and at once he made plans to join her there. He telephoned Croydon to charter a private aircraft to pick him up in Paris and fly him to North Africa.

One couple turned up to be married in full punk regalia. The man wearing bondage trousers, spikey hair and safety pins, while his bride was dressed from head to foot in black leather – but each of them had a red rose pinned to their breast. They, too, made the time-honoured visit to the blacksmith's shops, linking their modern image with those rebellious runaways of old times.

Some come totally on their own and want to be on their own with no fuss. They wear their everyday jeans and sweaters, 'But it's the eyes that tell so much,' said one lady, 'You can see it means so much to them, being like that, just as much as it does for the couple who come in full bridal regalia, top hat and tails, bridesmaids and all their relatives behind them.'

'It will cost a thousand pounds,' he was told.

'Send it – quick,' he ordered without hesitation.

Fog held up the plane in London and it was midnight when it touched down in Paris, at Orly Airport. Jimmy boarded it with two companions immediately. It taxied onto the runway where it was forced to wait as another plane, a Comet, was landing. As soon as it was clear, the charter plane roared off into the night. But, before the noise of its engines had died away, the passengers from the other plane were disembarking, and among them were Isabel and her chaperone. She had been delighted when, after only a few days in Morocco, her father sent for her to return to Paris immediately. Her joy was dashed when she found that Jimmy had gone.

Suddenly an opportunity of escape came when the vigilance of her chaperone and the detectives was momentarily relaxed. Flinging on her leopardskin coat, grabbing her passport and without even an overnight bag, Isabel managed to leave her father's mansion without being seen. She found a taxi and ordered the driver to race to Orly Airport. She phoned a friend to meet her in London and caught the next scheduled flight.

The friend had a car waiting for Isabel and they drove to his house. He told her where Jimmy was – in Morocco, searching for her. At once she phoned the hotel in Casablanca and got through to him.

'I'm in London. I've got away from them all.'

'Wait there.' He was as excited as she was. 'Don't move an inch. I'll jump into my plane this minute – on my way.'

In a few hours they were together again and they lost no time in putting their plans into action. They left London in a chauffeur driven Rolls Royce on Saturday, 12 December 1953, heading northwards. They stopped briefly at the Grosvenor Arms Hotel at Aldford, where Jimmy's brother and sister-in-law were staying. Both Jimmy and Isabel were bubbling with excitement and laughter as they told Edward and Jill that they were off to Scotland to get married.

'We'll let you know when and where,' they said gaily, as the car drove off.

Four hundred miles north, on the night of 13 December, they arrived in Edinburgh. Isabel went to stay at Carnock Lodge, the home of a respectable lawyer, Mr James L Mounsey and his wife, in Churchill Crescent. Jimmy stayed in a bungalow in Drylaw Crescent with Mr and Mrs Charles Sinclair. Mrs Sinclair's sympathy was easily aroused for the handsome young man and the beautiful girl, both so very much in love.

By 29 December the necessary residential period in Scotland had been complied with, and they called at the Register Office in each of the districts in which they were staying, to give notice of their intention to marry. Their names were only two among many on the type-written announcement which was then displayed outside both buildings.

James Michael Goldsmith, Bachelor, Hotelier.
14 Drylaw Crescent, Blackhall.
and
Isabel Patino, Spinster.
14 Churchill Crescent, Edinburgh.

Any objection to the marriage had to be lodged within seven days, and with that public display of their intention to marry, Señor and Señora Patino at last had an idea of the whereabouts of their daughter. They flew immediately to London and caught the overnight train to Edinburgh, where Don Antenor set up his headquarters in a three-room suite at the Caledonian Hotel.

By that time, however, Jimmy and Isabel had left the city and no one would divulge where they had gone. Don Antenor filed a petition for an interim interdict to prevent the two Edinburgh registrars from issuing the marriage licences and Lord Birnam, the vacation judge, granted the postponement. Señor Patino insisted that Isabel was domiciled in France, and therefore could not marry without his consent until she was twenty-one. The plea entered for him was worded thus: 'It is easier for a marriage to be stopped than to undo it. Can a marriage under Scottish law be regarded as valid in continental countries?'

The Patino millions were made available to pay private detectives who

Mr Rennison recalled in 'The Gretna Blacksmith's Story', that on one occasion he was quite shocked to find himself marrying a bride who wore no stockings! The jaunty young lady and stylishly-dressed gentleman had arrived by car just as a newly married couple walked out of the marriage room.

'Have you been getting married?' the newly arrived young lady asked, and on hearing that the other couple had, she said, 'I'm going in to be married, too.'

Mr Rennison took stock of her. She was fashionably dressed in light fawn, with salmon coloured streamers. She wore a stylish pair of shoes – but though he looked hard, he could see no stockings. At the anvil he said she acted with the greatest aplomb, but he remained a trifle disconcerted. 'I have married people in all sorts of guises,' he wrote, 'but this was the first and only time a bare-legged bride stepped out of the old Smithy.'

desperately tried to trace the runaways. Newspaper reporters were alerted all over Scotland and the whole world's Press awaited their reports. Meanwhile Jimmy and Isabel moved from place to place, dodging about Scotland, helped by friends and well-wishers. From Edinburgh they drove to Berwick, the next day to Linlithgow and then to Stirling, where they booked into the Golden Lion Hotel just before lunch. Boldly they signed their own names in the register, booked two single rooms and stayed there over Hogmanay. The Rolls had been replaced by a Standard Vanguard, which Jimmy drove himself. New Year's Day was spent in Perth. They had two days at the Drummond Arms, in Crieff, then moved on to Kelty in Fife, where they lodged in a fifty-room mansion, Blairadam. The owner was Captain C K Adam, a retired naval officer who said later, 'Their solicitor is an old friend of mine and he telephoned and asked if I could put up a young couple within the hour. He didn't say who they were, but I had a good idea.'

Isabel was cold and tired when they arrived but with a warm welcome and a warm meal, she soon relaxed. The children of their host helped them to pass the time by playing card games. But they dared not stay long in any one place for the threat that the detectives hired by Señor Patino might find them and forcibly carry Isabel back to her father, was ever present. She remembered all too clearly what had happened to Christina only a year or two before. They drove right across Scotland

and, on the day before the court was to consider its verdict, stayed on the banks of Loch Awe.

On 7 January 1954, the Court of Session in Edinburgh prepared to hear the Patino case, which had been classified as 'urgent'. The petition argued that, according to the law of France, Isabel had no right to decide whom she married. Minors could not enter a marriage contract without the consent of their father and mother. It was on that point that Don Antenor's case rested. Mr J C Young, the Scottish Registrar-General's deputy and an expert on Scottish marriage practice for over forty years, made his views clear to the Press, 'It has never been suggested to us that anything but Scottish Law obtains in these matters, here.'

The case was never fought out for Señor Patino abandoned his petition. The interdict against the issue of the licence was withdrawn quite unexpectedly on the very morning it was due to be heard. Perhaps that decision did not entirely surprise Jimmy and Isabel, for they had taken great care to ascertain their rights under Scottish law. Besides, on that same morning, in a quiet place in the Highlands, hiding in the back of a pig-van, they had kept a secret rendezvous with Isabel's mother. She gave them her blessing.

At 2 pm the marriage licences were collected by a solicitor. Later that afternoon Isabel, accompanied by her lawyer, arrived at the Ednam Hotel in Kelso. Small, dark, vivacious and radiant, she talked excitedly to everyone around her. What a different wedding it was to that of her sister and Prince Marc de Beauvau-Craon, just a couple of years earlier! That had been at the Church of St Louis des Invalides in Paris, and Christina had had difficulty in coping with a twenty-foot long train of satin, eleven feet wide, with an overlay of needlepoint lace. For her simple Scottish wedding, Isabel wore a yellow woollen twin set with a grey skirt and she carried a bouquet of lilies of the valley. She had spurned many eligible royal suitors to marry the man of her choice.

They were married by Mr James Maule, Registrar of the little border town in Roxburghshire, the town which Sir Walter Scott described as 'the most picturesque and romantic village in Scotland'. The ceremony, taking the usual quarter of an hour, was witnessed by their two solicitors, Captain Smith and Mr Edward Doughty. Then, thankful that it was over, and that at last their need to hide was over, they got into the car. A small crowd had gathered and as they drove away towards Edinburgh, Isabel waved and waved, and the world was delighted for them. Love, aided by the straightforward honesty of the marriage laws of Scotland, had not been broken by all the wealth in the world.

They stayed overnight at 'a quiet guesthouse', Prestonfield House, on the outskirts of Edinburgh and strolled through the grounds beneath the slope of Arthur's Seat. Jimmy's father, Major Frank Goldsmith, sent a

One of the most strangely dressed couples that Miss Bryden recalls were Americans. The groom wore an immaculate white suit, the bride carried a large bag. She asked for somewhere to change, and was shown into an ante-room. Miss Bryden assumed she would be putting on a white gown, but when she saw her she was flabbergasted. The bride was dressed as Donald Duck!

telegram saying 'My wife and I are overjoyed. All's well that ends well.'

There was no immediate greeting from Señor Patino, who hurried silently through the throng of reporters with his wife; they left Scotland by train, accompanied by solicitors and detectives. He had to run the same gauntlet again when he arrived in London but had nothing to say.

Next day Jimmy and Isabel gave a lunch at the George Hotel in Edinburgh, and there, as the health of the bride and groom were toasted in champagne, Mr Sinclair voiced the feelings of all his countrymen when he said, 'This young couple came to us and we took them to our hearts. Everyone has been so touched by their romance.' No one could have any inkling of how short a time the young couple would have to share their happiness.

Wearing her leopardskin coat but now also a plain gold wedding ring, Isabel left on the train from Waverley Station that evening with her husband. A few days later they returned to Paris. It was then Don Antenor telephoned his daughter and said, 'Remember I'm always your father. If you need anything, come to me.'

Blissfully happy at that time, there was nothing that Isabel wanted, and as the months passed, and she became sure that she was pregnant, her happiness increased. They rented a small apartment in a hotel next to the Pompadour Room; Jimmy got back to work at his office overlooking the Opera. Often they dined at a modest restaurant in Montmartre. Twice they took trips to the South of France and Jimmy went to the casino and won. He smiled at Isabel saying, 'I was born lucky, but you have made me luckier.'

On 15 May, Isabel went to have tea with her father, as she did quite regularly. He still refused to accept his new son-in-law, and the two families had not yet met, but Isabel hoped that before long there would be a complete reconciliation. Afterwards she met Jimmy in the Pompadour Room and they went to a bistro near the Sacré Coeur for dinner. Isabel seemed perfectly well when she went to bed, but at four o'clock she woke up complaining of a headache. Jimmy fetched her a glass of water. She was asleep when he went to his office, so he did not wake her. Later that morning Mrs Goldsmith, Jimmy's mother, who was living in a suite in the same hotel, went to call on Isabel and found her unconscious.

Immediately she was rushed to hospital. It was a brain haemorrhage. Two delicate operations were performed as eminent surgeons fought to save her life. The baby, a girl, was delivered by Caesarian section, but her lovely young mother never recovered consciousness. The premature baby, also called Isabel, weighed only 3½lbs and she was placed at once in an oxygen tent at the Paris clinic; no one thought she would survive.

Señor Patino flew into Paris, as did Jimmy's father. All were helpless. Isabel died the following morning. Her body was taken from the hospital to her father's mansion.

The funeral stopped the traffic in the city, as hundreds of women crowded, weeping, around the Church of St Honore d'Eylau in the fashionable Avenue Hoche and the police had to struggle to keep places for the members of the Patino and Goldsmith families. A choir and orchestra of sixty musicians accompanied the Requiem Mass. Don Antenor Patino, looking a fragile little man, followed his grief-stricken son-in-law. It was the first time since the elopement that the two families had come together but reconciliation was not yet complete.

For James Goldsmith another battle against Don Antenor and his wife lay ahead. Immediately after Isabel's death, Jimmy agreed that Madam Patino should look after the delicate baby. In his sorrow he could not think too far ahead but threw himself into his business commitments and took a long trip to Africa. When he returned the Patinos were unwilling to relinquish the child, and they applied to the court for summary judgement for custody, implying that Jimmy's flat in Paris was unsuitable. He was determined to keep his daughter and he had no doubt that that would have been Isabel's wish also. He went at once to the Patino mansion in Versailles but the baby and her nurse had both gone. There was no other course than for him to institute legal proceedings to regain custody of baby Isabel. It took a long time, but finally he won.

Isabel grew more and more like her mother and she never looked more so than on her wedding day in June 1973. Then, on the arm of her father, by this time Sir James Goldsmith, Isabel Goldsmith looked just as radiant and shyly happy as Isabel Patino had twenty years before. Over the years Sir James Goldsmith became fully reconciled with Don Antenor Patino.

What an inspiration that elopement was to hundreds of frustrated young lovers! Why should they wait three or four years to marry because they were under twenty-one and their parents refused to give consent?

---

Again Miss Bryden was somewhat taken aback when a couple walked into her office dressed as Mickey and Minnie Mouse – followed by their witnesses in the costumes of Rupert Bear and Kermit the Frog! Pat has a reputation for being unflappable, but this was so bizarre she felt obliged to question their attitude, saying she hoped they were not intending to make a farce of the wedding.

'Oh, no,' they replied. 'We just like Minnie and Mickey Mouse.'

'But what will you think when you look back and see your wedding photographs? And what will your children say?'

'Oh, they'll probably like it, too,' was the answer.

They insisted they were serious, and certainly they had made all the arrangements correctly and the marriage was solemnised as usual.

Afterwards they said, 'We got so bored with looking at friends' wedding albums, which always seemed so much alike, we decided to do something different.'

CHAPTER THIRTEEN

# Runaways of the Fifties and Sixties

The Register Office in Gretna was opened in the summer of 1940, in a small new building on the Annan Road, close to the shopping centre. During its first few years there was nothing particularly remarkable in the number of births, marriages and deaths registered there. That changed when, as the year turned from 1953 to 1954, every newspaper in the country was blazoned with the romance of Jimmy Goldsmith and Isabel Patino!

Their story revealed to the whole world that a simple wedding service in Scotland was still available, that it was absolutely legal and binding, and that even the richest parent in the world could not bring an injunction to stop it. The details were in all the papers. A couple had only to complete the necessary residential qualification and give notification, and the wedding could be conducted in any Register Office in Scotland. That last piece of information was virtually ignored. In the following decade and a half, thousands of couples eloped – and the majority of them headed straight for Gretna Green.

The appetite of the press for romantic stories had been whetted, and for the next few years every runaway wedding was treated as front page news. One national daily got so excited it embellished the stories of the first couple or two by providing a Rolls Royce and all the trimmings of a slap-up wedding. Before long hundreds of young couples were pouring into Gretna.

Among those who eloped in 1956 were Ann Bott and Ray Searle. They had bumped into each other – quite literally – at a roller-skating rink in Coventry about a year previously. From then on they met regularly, and before long they were going out together every evening.

Quite early in their courtship Ray asked Ann, 'If we had to run away – would you?'

'Yes,' she answered. But she never dreamed that it would actually come to that.

Ann was not quite seventeen and Ray only eighteen when, sure that they wanted to spend the rest of their lives together, they decided to ask their parents for consent to marry. Determined to do the thing properly, Ray called at Ann's home. He had taken care to make himself smart and tidy, hoping to impress her parents by looking his best, and because the occasion demanded such formality. Her parents courteously invited him into the front room. The atmosphere was tense as, with simple sincerity, he told them he wished to marry their daughter. Mr and Mrs Bott murmured that he and Ann were still rather young – but they liked Ray and to his delight they presented little opposition. Feeling on top of the world, Ann and Ray went to speak to his parents.

'You haven't done anything silly?' asked Mrs Searle, her first reaction being to imagine that Ann was pregnant.

'No, it's not that,' Ray said quickly. 'We just want to get married.'

His parents were not at all happy about the idea. For one thing, Ray would soon be called up for National Service and both Mr and Mrs Searle felt it would be wiser to wait until he had finished that. Ray's mother was particularly against their marrying. She was convinced they were too young and nothing they said would persuade her to change her mind. She absolutely refused to give her consent. It would have been quite alien to the mores of their time for them simply to leave home and live together. They never even discussed such an outrageous idea. They began to plan their elopement.

It took about a month. They drew all their savings out of the Post Office, taking a small amount each day because if they drew more than two pounds, the books would be sent away to head office. This meant they would be posted back to their homes and their mothers would have noticed and asked questions. As they collected the pound notes together Ray hid them under the lino in his bedroom.

The week before they left, they bought the wedding ring. The last evening was spent writing letters to their parents, it was not easy to find the right words but it had to be done. The gist of the letters was 'Don't worry when we don't come home tonight. We've gone to Scotland to get married and will be home in about three weeks' time.'

On the appointed morning they each left home at their usual time, as if going to work. Ray posted his letter confident that it would be delivered that same afternoon and Ann left hers with a girlfriend, asking her to hand it to her mother at tea-time but not letting her know what was in it. Ray, who was employed on a building site, had his overalls over his suit and looked exceedingly bulbous when he met Ann at the corner of the street. She worked as a telephone assembler. They could take very little with them except what extra clothes they could put on. There had been a breath-stopping moment for Ray when he found his mother

In May 1961 a seventeen-year-old German youth, Dieter Malbe yearned to marry his eighteen-year-old sweetheart, Dietrum, but his mother forbad the match. Gretna Green was the young lovers only hope, so they eloped from their homes at Bad Rappenau, near Stuttgart.

They hitch-hiked from the ferry and spent what little money they had on renting a caravan on a local site in order to fulfil the statutory residential qualification. That left them practically penniless. Dieter's family tried, through Interpol, to get local police to intervene and stop the marriage, but Scots law prevailed and the couple were wed.

Since then life has improved for Herr and Frau Malbe, they now run a prosperous guest house and restaurant in Bad Rappenau, and Dieter's family have long since given their blessing to the match. They have three children. Their eldest, Gordon, was named after a Moffat hotelier, Mr Gordon Hamilton, who heard of their plight and gave them £30 to buy food.

In 1978, the runaways fulfilled an ambition to return to the village where they had been married by Mr Bob Hastings, who was then Registrar. They came back in very different style, driving a Mercedes, and memories flooded back as they made a nostalgic tour of the village and were shown round the famous Old Blacksmith's Shop which they had visited after their wedding, by the proprietor, Mr Adair Houston.

'It is wonderful to be back,' said Dieter. 'The first time we came we had little money, and were sometimes miserable. But on this visit we are very happy and are glad to see some of the people who were so friendly to us then.'

hunting for some matches in the pocket of his raincoat! She took out his razor but by good luck was too preoccupied to question why he had put it there. At the station Ray took off his overalls and put them in a left luggage locker. Then they boarded the train for Carlisle.

'The funny thing was at the end of the trip we didn't quite know what had happened since we left home,' Ann remembered with a smile. 'Quite a few hours had gone from the time we left Coventry, and as the train pulled into Carlisle, we began to panic in case anybody had contacted the police. We got off the train by separate doors and went out of the station by different exits, so nobody would see us as a couple who had travelled together. We met up again outside the station. We imagined every policeman in town would be looking for us. But of course, nobody was even bothered!'

Ann and Ray found lodgings quite easily. 'I think at that time it was almost like a business, the minute you got into Gretna, people knew. There were quite a lot of young couples in the village, waiting to get married. We asked at the fish and chip shop and they gave us some addresses.' At first Ray stayed in a different house to Ann but after a week there was a spare bed in her lodgings so he was able to move in. He shared a room with the landlady's grandson. 'People were very good to us,' Ann said. 'And the police seemed to keep a check that people who took in runaways looked after them properly. Our landlady was a sweet old Scots lady called Maggie. She was a super cook – I got quite hooked on her Scots pancakes.'

The next day they went to the Register Office and made arrangements for the wedding. They also wrote home to let their parents know exactly where they were. After that it was a matter of settling down to wait for the necessary three weeks or twenty-four days to be exact, because Sundays were not included. In common with most of the couples there was little money to spare for luxuries, just a few pence each day for a newspaper and a mid-morning cup of coffee. The afternoon was spent walking or fishing, and there Ray was lucky, because Maggie's grandson knew all the best spots for catching trout in the Sark.

After about a week they received letters from their parents, the gist of which was: 'Come home. All is forgiven. You can get married here since you are obviously so determined.' But, by that time they felt they would rather stay on and be married at Gretna anyway. When their mothers received that reply they both decided to make the best of it, and wrote to say they would travel up to Scotland and would like to be witnesses at the wedding. Ann and Ray feel they were very fortunate in knowing so early after their elopement that they had not become totally estranged from home, for that was a risk that every eloping couple took.

Runaways were still very much the news; Ann and Ray took part in a television documentary while they were waiting for their wedding and to their delight they were paid a fee of £10. It was not only Scottish and English television companies that filmed the Gretna scene, several crews also arrived from the Continent to get their various versions of the story.

During the next few years the numbers of runaways increased – alarmingly so in the view of some people. By the early 1960s couples were coming to Gretna in great numbers, not only from England, but from all over Europe and some from more distant parts of the world. In most of Europe the age of majority was twenty-one, but in some countries it was older than that, and in Holland, for example, it was

In 1976 the first Chinese couple were married in Gretna. Kwan Sue Chung, a cook, aged thirty-one and his bride, Yuen Wa Hui, aged twenty-six, came from Lancashire, wisely bringing an interpreter with them.

thirty. Several were in their late twenties and there were also a few middle-aged people who had special problems over documentation. Often parents were in pursuit. They would call upon the police to locate errant sons or daughters but since they were not breaking Scottish law, no charges could be laid against them. The sympathy of local residents often seemed to lie with the youngsters, as parents chased them around Scotland, but there was also increasing concern about the reputation that such behaviour gave to their village. The council, in an attempt to stop the flood, made a byelaw for their tenants in local authority housing, forbidding them from providing accommodation. It was hoped that if there was nowhere to stay, the runaways would give up and go back home. It made no difference, they were made of sterner stuff than that. It also allowed private enterprise to swing into action.

The Press began to change its emphasis. Words of romance dried up on their pens and they began to seek out the sleasier side of the situation, and used emotive headlines such as 'Village of Shame'. In the year 1961, 365 couples were married at Gretna Register Office, and an article, published in August the following year, reported that fifty-eight couples were 'mooching around the dull, distraction-free village'. It highlighted the worries of Gretna parents who said that little girls no longer played at houses but had invented a game called 'runaway couples'. The boys, instead of train-spotting, turned their activities to 'runaway-spotting' in lonely haunts by the river, on the railway embankment or in the surrounding fields. The young couples of that decade were no different from those of five or six years earlier, who had been so courted by the Press, it was simply that there were so many of them.

The wedding of Pat and Michael Ware on 14 June 1962 was witnessed by a Dutch sailor, who was in Gretna waiting to marry a girl from Harwich. 'There were so many foreigners in Gretna at that time it seemed quite difficult to find an English couple to witness the marriage for us. But it did not matter what their nationality was,' Pat said.

She was then eighteen and Michael was nineteen. They had been going out together for almost two years and had been engaged for eight months, but Pat's father did not approve of Mike. He told his daughter quite definitely, 'You're not getting married.' He refused even to discuss the matter further, and Pat knew there was no hope that he would change his mind. His refusal meant they would have to wait for three years, until she came of age, and they were not prepared to do that. In January they began to plan their elopement. They left home in May.

'Both our mothers went out to work,' Pat said. 'That made things easier, but I dared not leave home carrying a suitcase, because on our block of flats I'd have been seen and it would have started a rumour immediately. We'd done most of the planning when we spent evenings together in the front room of Michael's parents' house. They thought we were just listening to records but we were working out ways and means. Every evening when I went round to see him, I took one or two things, perhaps an extra dress or a couple of pairs of pants, and Mike packed them all in a big holdall under his bed.

'Michael's boss was the only person who knew we were going. He was a butcher and he helped us to get to the station, and we knew he'd give Mike his job back afterwards. Apart from that we had no idea how we would make out in future. Our parents could just have slammed the doors in our faces and said, "You've made your bed, so you must lie on it." We wrote our farewell notes and tried to put it as tactfully as we could. I left mine on the table, as I might have done if I'd written to say that I'd be late for dinner. It must have been a terrible shock when they realised that this time I was writing to say I would be back in three weeks and by then I'd be married.'

In Gretna, Pat and Mike found a small hotel and booked two single rooms for bed and breakfast. At first they lived in fear that their parents might seek them out, especially as Mike's father was a long-distance lorry driver. It never happened to them but there were other dramas. Pat recalled, 'One night I heard a bit of a rumpus at about three o'clock in the morning. I couldn't make out what was going on, but next morning we heard that a girl had been kidnapped during the night.

'Her parents had come and they'd asked to see her, and she'd agreed to go outside and talk to them, and they'd just bundled her into the car and took her home. I was sorry for her fellow. He didn't know till he went to knock on her door the next morning. He left the hotel, went off to try and find her, but I've no idea how things turned out.

'We'd been there about a couple of weeks when we received a letter from Mike's parents to say we could live with them until we got a place of our own. That was marvellous news. After that we could really relax and enjoy being in Gretna.

'It was a simple way of life. It had to be, with so little money, but we were better off than some. Those who could not afford an hotel stayed in caravans or tents. There were lots of couples, and everyone was really friendly.' Pat remembered a 'super transport café where we had a really fantastic meal, with masses to eat and plenty of tea and bread and butter. Unfortunately we only discovered it on our last day there. Most afternoons we just went for a walk. That day the manager suggested we should walk down to the sea.

'We said – "What sea? We've been here almost three weeks and we haven't seen any sea."

'He was talking about the Solway. We walked down and it was beautiful! A cold windy day and the sea seemed to be all around you, absolutely lovely!' The weather was wet and windy for their wedding. 'I wore an ordinary dress, one I'd just taken with me, but I'd saved it for the wedding. It was hardly suitable, just a straight sleeveless cotton frock. I'd have liked a new dress, but that wasn't possible.'

They were so broke when they arrived back they did not even have enough money for the bus fare from the station. They had to telephone a friend who picked them up and took them to Michael's home. Pat told me, 'My father always said our marriage wouldn't last, and everyone thought I must be pregnant, but I disappointed them by waiting for two years before I produced my daughter.

'I think one of the factors about Gretna marriages in those days, was that once you'd taken such a big step, you'd just got to make a success of it. You didn't know what the reaction would be when you got back. I wasn't even sure that my job would be kept for me. People are convinced that a runaway marriage won't last, and you have to work at it to make sure that it does. It wasn't something we did lightly, and I wouldn't like to think I'd gone through all that for nothing. We've had our ups and downs, but we soon get back together. I'd do it again if I had to.'

Another runaway bride at about that time was Janice Hartgill. She met Dave Cooper when they were on holiday in Bognor Regis where they were staying in caravans with their respective parents. It was their mothers who first started chatting, and when Dave's mother suggested he should make friends with Jan, he was not at all keen. He had already decided from a distance that he didn't like the look of her.

Later, however, he noticed her in the nearby amusement arcade. She had been trying to put a penny into a machine and it was stuck, so Dave went over and helped her. They spent the rest of that evening together, met again the next morning and then every day for the rest of the week. Even before the holiday was over they had decided they would marry, though Jan was then barely sixteen and Dave only eighteen months older.

During the following year they wrote or phoned every day, not easy as neither of them was on the telephone and they had to use public call boxes. Soon they were spending every weekend together, alternately at

139

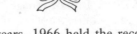

For almost eighteen years, 1966 held the record for the greatest number of marriages in one year at Gretna, 521 couples. That was in the heyday of the runaway marriages. It was not beaten until August 1984 when Bill Brindle and his bride, Margaret Brow, arrived at the Register Office, and became the 522nd couple to be married that year.

Margaret wore an Edwardian dress of cream lace and a gorgeously frothy hat, but neither of them knew they were making history with their wedding. Friends in Carlisle had loaned them a pony and trap for the day but when they drove up in such style, they had no idea they would be met by a posse of reporters and photographers.

'We came to Gretna because it seemed the most romantic thing to do,' said Margaret.

Jan's home or at Dave's, thirty miles away. The following May they got engaged, but both lots of parents insisted they were too young to marry, so they decided to elope.

Plans took them about six weeks and Jan had to send away for a duplicate of Dave's birth certificate, as he did not know where his mother kept his and he dared not ask her for it. They bought a wedding ring and Jan made herself a plain white dress. Dave gave up his job saying he was going to leave the country, which they reckoned was basically true. They each told their parents that they were going to stay for a week's holiday at the home of the other. Jan's father carried her suitcase to the station and remarked, 'It feels heavy enough for a month!'

Neither Jan nor Dave was clear where Gretna was, they only knew it was in Scotland. They boarded the Edinburgh train, and only discovered when they arrived that they were on the wrong side of the country and a good many miles further north than they intended. Nor did they know they could just as easily get married in Edinburgh, or anywhere else in Scotland, they believed it had to be Gretna. It was the middle of August, during the Festival, and the only place in Edinburgh they could find to stay was in a guesthouse where they were told they could sleep in the dining-room. They didn't dare say they were runaways so they said they'd just got married. Then it seemed as if everyone was looking at them, and they were treated as if they were a honeymoon couple. The TV was switched off and the other guests hurried out of the room, so that the 'wee bairns could get to bed'.

Next morning they took the train back to Carlisle and thence to Gretna where they booked in at the Lover's Leap Motel. They called at the Register Office and learned exactly how long they would have to stay – and realised they would definitely have to find cheaper accommodation. All the boarding-houses seemed to be fully booked, but at last Jan and Dave managed to rent one room in a so-called cottage in the back garden of a small hotel. It was part of an asbestos hut with a corrugated roof. 'More like a chicken-hut,' Dave described it. It had two camp beds with straw mattresses and a chest of drawers. There was only one lavatory and one washbasin for about four couples. A German couple were in the next room and every time they went in and out they had to go through the one that Jan and Dave rented. 'He would come through in his paisley pyjamas, and she in her frilly nightie,' Jan laughed. The German fräulein was evidently pregnant, but Jan and Dave had no chance to hear their story because they could not communicate in each other's languages. Each couple did their own cooking on a primus stove, and Dave can still recall the continual smell of garlic from next door. After about a week they managed to move into half a caravan, which was definitely better and more private.

Jan and Dave recalled an occasion when they had unthinkingly gone to Carlisle with another couple. The girl went to the savings bank because she had arranged to draw out some money. The cashier kept them waiting and went into the back of the bank. He returned, and as he paid over the money, two detectives came into the bank and took charge of the girl. Because her bank book had been sent home, her parents had been able to contact the police and as she was then in England, they were able to hold her and send for her parents. Had she stayed in Scotland that could not have happened. Considerably shaken, Jan and Dave caught the next bus out of Carlisle. In fact they were never pursued, but there was always a fear that something could happen at any time to thwart their plans, and they never ventured south of the border again until after they were married.

Towards the end of the first week, knowing that they would soon be expected home from their supposed 'holidays', they each wrote to their parents telling them where they were. On tenterhooks they waited for replies, very conscious of the shock they had sprung on their loving parents. Mrs Hartgill recovered quite quickly and decided she was not going to miss the wedding of her only daughter, rebel though she might be. She travelled overnight in order to be in Gretna on the day.

Jan and Dave were married at 9.15 am on 4 September 1963 and afterwards they took Mrs Hartgill to look around the Blacksmith's Shop. There Jan's mother noticed a photographer taking pictures of a mock wedding being performed for some Americans. She told him she would like a photograph of her daughter and son-in-law. Jan took off her coat and at once her white dress was spotted by one of the tourists, who asked, 'Say – are you a real bride?' So Jan and Dave had to pose, clasping hands through the lucky horseshoe by the anvil, while cameras clicked all around them. When they went back home, reporters were waiting for their train and their picture and their story was given wide coverage in the local paper.

It is with mixed feelings that the people of Gretna look back on those years. One man said, 'There were hundreds of them about. The young couples were everywhere. Those that could not get rooms pitched tents anywhere they could find a space, and when the weather was really bad, they moved in under railway bridges, or into chicken huts.' With grudging admiration, he added, 'My goodness, some of them really did have it rough!' He recalled one couple who slept in plastic bags under the hedges, and came into town just to buy a loaf of bread because that was all they could afford; it was a particularly wet and cold summer that year, yet they stuck it out until their wedding day.

The very numbers of the runaways created a nuisance. Many local people felt they ought not to condone the way the youngsters were flouting the wishes of their parents. Some couples were condemned for their lack of moral values, and also there was some disgust at the fact that a few local people exploited them. Yet overlying all that, there remains a guarded admiration. It is remembered that although most of them were desperately hard up, they stayed on for over three weeks, no matter what happened, because they were so determined to be married. No one can recall any couple who gave up voluntarily.

The newspapers now asserted that there was little glamour in the 'bedraggled young couples'. They searched the byways for photographs of the sloppiest and reported another new game for the village children. This was to watch a couple slowly walking along in a deep embrace and time their kiss to see how long it could last. Yet again there was agitation for a change in the law, and all the old arguments were trotted out once more. Some felt that the age of marriage without parental consent in Scotland should be raised. Others argued that the law was still no problem to the Scots, it had served them very well as it had for centuries, and they had no wish to have it altered. The main contention continued to be that somehow it should be made more difficult, if not impossible, for foreigners to take advantage of it.

The number of weddings in Gretna built up steadily until a peak in 1966, with 521 weddings. They included just about every nationality in the world. For some couples, especially those from Europe, the Scottish marriage laws provided a way out of really desperate trouble. For example there were a couple of Czechs, both middle aged, living in West

Germany, who had lost all their personal papers while they were in concentration camps. They were married in church in Poland, but church weddings are not recognised by the state in West Germany and without papers they could not be legally married so they could get none of the status generally accorded to married couples. Only by going to Scotland could they be legally married and attain their full rights. Similarly, a fifty-year-old Italian, working in Germany and divorced from his Italian wife, was unable to remarry in West Germany. German law allowed him to divorce but could not allow him to remarry, because under Italian law, the divorce was not acceptable. He came to Scotland with his German fräulein to be married and this was perfectly legal. In Holland, where there is a large Catholic community, permission was rarely given for mixed marriages. If a Catholic fell in love with a Protestant, there was little chance of parental consent being given and that meant waiting until they were over thirty. For people such as these a Scottish wedding presented the only possible solution.

Financial considerations also played their part. In some European families, the earnings of grown-up sons and daughters were expected to be handed over intact, and they were then given back some pocket money. Consent to a marriage might be refused simply to keep this money in the parents' hands. One girl's father had recently bought a car on hire purchase. He relied on her earnings to pay the instalments, so he refused his permission for her to marry even though she was in her mid-twenties. She escaped to Gretna.

One young Belgian of twenty-four, who came with his nineteen-year-old girlfriend, was arrested by the police on a charge of abducting her. Their landlady, who spoke fluent French, knew that the girl had come of her own free will but such was the power and pressure of her parents that the boy was arrested and taken to Brixton prison in London. The girl was advised to go to her embassy. This she could easily have done, but she feared that such a move would put her under Belgian law and she chose to stay where she was, living in a tent on a campsite in Gretna. Well-wishers employed the services of a Scottish lawyer to plead the young man's innocence and before long he was released. He arrived back at the camp at 2 am, dodging reporters, who were there in full force, trying to get his story. The couple were married the next morning and returned to their own country. Despite so much harassment they have since been reconciled to their parents, have a successful and happy marriage, children, a lovely home, and their Scottish landlady visits them sometimes when she is in Belgium.

Various subterfuges have been employed by parents seeking to get their recalcitrant offspring back under their control. One case involved a man who had been a Roman Catholic priest but had left the ministry,

It was 1985 when the record was broken again when over one thousand weddings took place at the Gretna Register Office – and that number was reached by September. The couple who made the record arrived quite unsuspectingly. Robert Simpson and Brenda Ling both originated from England, but were living in Glasgow. They expected to make only a brief stop at Gretna, get married quietly and then continue on their way south to visit their families. But as they walked out of the door after their marriage, they were met not only by a barrage of reporters and photographers, but also by many local business people.

The Director of Tourism presented them with a bottle of malt whisky and a 'Scotland for me' garter, and promised them a free holiday in the region on their first anniversary. They were whisked away to Gretna Hall for a reception, and had to turn down a similar offer from the Gretna Chase Hotel. Photographs were given free, and officials from Annandale and Eskdale District Council presented them with the coat of arms of the area.

They were totally overwhelmed by the lavishness of the arrangements that had been made for them – so different from the quiet ceremony they had planned.

returned to secular life and had become a university professor. He fell in love with one of his students, a girl from a very rich family, when he was forty-two and the girl was twenty-two. Permission to marry was refused and they eloped to Gretna. The family followed and tried to prevent the marriage by every means in their power. They even attempted to have the man certified insane when they learned that this was one of the few considerations which might enable them to stop the wedding.

Another story concerns a father who lived on the immoral earnings of his daughters, and was so reluctant to lose the services of one of them that he would not consent to her marriage. Sadder was the story of the only daughter of an invalid mother, who was terrified of her father. She 'acted like a frightened rabbit', cowered in her tent and seemed to be scared to leave the camp site. She was often seen to be crying. Eventually the landlady discovered that since she had been in her early teens her father had demanded her services in the place of those the invalid mother was unable to give him. Her father came from the Continent in search of her and when the police did not believe her story, she did not have the strength to withstand the pressure on her and allowed herself to be taken home. The true story came into the open when she was taken into a home for wayward girls as being beyond the control of her parents.

Those couples who came in the winter and lived under canvas, endured great hardships. To reach Gretna from the Continent was not a trip to be lightly undertaken. The English couples who travelled there had to plan and save for several weeks, but those from Europe had to raise even more money for their fares, yet hundreds of them managed it, determined against all the odds to marry for love. Many couples return on holiday visits, and as the years go on, they bring their children and grandchildren with them. Almost all retain vivid and happy recollections of the village, and especially of the places where they stayed. They remember clearly every small incident, and are ever grateful for any small kindnesses they received. It was not easy for any of them, but now they can look back with laughter at so many of the funny and dramatic events of those memorable three weeks.

# CHAPTER FOURTEEN

# The Gretna Story Continues

Yet again there was a change in the law, a very sweeping one, which affected the whole of the United Kingdom. On 1 January 1970, the age of maturity was lowered from twenty-one to eighteen, and among the rights and responsibilities thus conferred was that of marrying without parental consent.

No longer was there any need for young adults of eighteen, nineteen or twenty to elope to Scotland, they could marry in their own home towns. The graph of marriages at Gretna dropped dramatically. For some years continental couples continued to arrive, but eventually legislation in most European countries was brought into line with the new thinking, and their citizens are now treated as adults after celebrating their eighteenth birthdays. In the United Kingdom it was only for the sixteen and seventeen-year-olds that the law north of the border differed meaningfully.

There still remain some Europeans for whom the laws of their own countries in some way constitute an impediment to their marrying. Many of these men and women find that a Scottish marriage provides the only possible solution for them, and the first place that springs into their minds (some say the only place they have ever heard of in Scotland) is Gretna. The number of applications from foreigners is nothing like as great now as it was in the fifties and sixties, but the registrar still has to be prepared to conduct many services every year for people who cannot speak any English.

'We must have an interpreter on those occasions, and we are fortunate that in Gretna there are people who speak several languages,' Miss Bryden explained. 'One Dutch lady speaks French, Dutch, Esperanto, German and Flemish, in fact she can cover all the countries bordering on Holland. Another lady is Flemish, and she speaks fluent French, German and Dutch and there is also an Italian lady who speaks several languages.

'Sometimes the continental weddings seem to take quite a long time. For instance, recently we had an Italian couple. The bride was only sixteen and so was too young to marry in her own country even though her parents were perfectly willing to give their consent, in fact her father and mother came with her. They all seemed to be chatting continually and then there was the interpreting, backwards and forwards. You must have a reliable interpreter to make sure that they have made the right vows and really understood them.'

In Gretna they keep a file with written interpretations for various languages – Dutch, French, Flemish, Italian, German, Spanish, Greek, Hindi, Chinese and Russian. For the ceremony with foreign couples, the registrar reads the paragraphs in English, the interpreter translates and then the couple read from the paper in their own language. In that way she can be certain that the couple really understand the service.

So well-known is Gretna for its marriages that any foreign letter which is strangely addressed is taken to the Register Office and more often than not, it is a request for information about marrying there. Miss Bryden has a suitcase filled with oddly inscribed envelopes from all over the world: to the Marriage People (where you elope to) Gretna Green, Scotland; Births, Deaths and Marriages; Mayor's Official Residence; The Mayor of Gretna Green; Home Office; Municipal Magistrate; Marriage Department; Mr Mayor of Gretna Green; Common House of Burghermaster; The Priest; The Ministry; Justice of the Peace; The Place to get Married, Gretna Green; Lady in Charge of the Marriage Shop. One strange letter which arrived in 1986 was addressed to 'Lord or Count of Gretna Green, near Dumfries, Écosse'. It was of course delivered to the Register Office and contained a letter from Ms Mascha Romanov, who was making enquiries about runaway marriages during the period 1754–1856. It set them wondering – was it from an exiled Russian princess? And what was her interest in runaways?

Yet another change in the law came with the Marriage (Scotland) Act 1977. This set aside the three weeks residential qualification which had been imposed under Lord Brougham's Act of 1857. Now all that is required is for applicants to write and give notice of their intention to marry. They must send the necessary forms and fees to the registrar in the three month period prior to the date of marriage, and not later than fifteen days before that date.

The big difference is that they do not need to attend in person. Their full names, but no other information, are displayed outside the Register Office. Such an easing of restrictions would undoubtedly have attracted greater numbers of foreigners than ever, so the new law included a condition that anyone from outside the United Kingdom who wished to be married in Scotland, must produce a certificate of no impediment.

'It does deter the young couples,' said Miss Bryden. 'The sixteen-year-olds coming here from the Continent, who may be under age in their own country. Now they have to produce this certificate, issued by their local registrar, to confirm that they have the consent of their parents. This also applies to divorcees, who must have a certificate in addition to the decree nisi absolute. It was introduced to cut down the continual run to Scotland.'

Once again the change brought a sharp upward trend in the number of marriages at Gretna, whilst other Register Offices in Scotland reported no increase. Despite the fact that the same law applies to all, the old mystique of the Village of Runaway Marriages remains. At first the weddings were mostly of older couples, people who had been living together for years, whose neighbours and friends knew them as Mr and Mrs. It was a simple way of changing their status officially. They could write and make the necessary arrangements, travel to Scotland, get married and go back home in one day, and their visit remained their secret.

But the change in the law also set the scene for a new wave of young couples, who began to be attracted by the idea of marrying in the most romantic place in the British Isles. Many are Scots but hundreds of young couples also travel there from England, Wales and Ireland, as well as from Europe and all over the world. Their numbers have been increasing since 1977.

In 1984, 900 couples were married and extra staff had to be recruited at the Register Office. Numbers shot up to well over a thousand in 1985, and since then they have continued at about capacity level; that is about fourteen hundred but when the new Register Office is built, it could easily increase.

When weddings over the anvil were made illegal in 1940, no one dreamed that a marriage would ever again take place in the famous Old Blacksmith's Shop. But on St Andrew's Day, 30 November 1985, that was where Wendy Rogerson and Neil McBride made their vows. It was very different from the old days of irregular marriages there because it was both legal and religious, and the service was conducted by a Church of Scotland minister.

It was a surprise, even to the bride herself, who expected the ceremony to take place in her home town of Dumfries. It wasn't until her wedding car headed out of town that she realised something unusual was happening, and only when they passed through Annan did it dawn on her that they might be going to Gretna.

Neil had planned the historic event with the help of Rev John Pagan, of St Michael's Church, Dumfries. About a dozen guests were assembled in the Smithy to await Wendy's arrival and join in the wedding

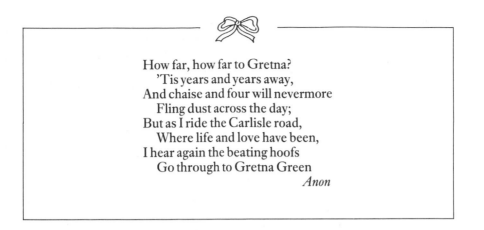

How far, how far to Gretna?
　　'Tis years and years away,
And chaise and four will nevermore
　　Fling dust across the day;
But as I ride the Carlisle road,
　　Where life and love have been,
I hear again the beating hoofs
　　Go through to Gretna Green
*Anon*

service. Wendy looked lovely in a white wedding gown and veil and Neil resplendent in Highland dress. A curtain was drawn across and sightseers were excluded during the actual ceremony but when the wedding party walked out a coachload of American tourists had just pulled in. They were there for the fun of a 'mock' wedding and were astounded to find that a real wedding had just been solemnised.

The bridegroom was South-West Scotland's stock car racing champion, and outside the old Smithy, to complete his amazing wedding arrangements, stood a 16-ton truck, decorated with white ribbons to take him and his bride to their reception back in Dumfries.

The Rev Pagan had been somewhat surprised when Neil approached him with his elaborate and unusual plans for his wedding, and he was prepared to give careful thought to the proposition. As a Church of Scotland minister he is entitled to marry anyone, at any time of the day or night, and in any place – even in a boat in the middle of a loch! It can be anywhere within the territorial waters of Scotland but he is not sure if it would be legal when flying in an aeroplane overhead. In the old days when people had little money, and little time for celebration, most marriages took place in the Manse, the minister's house, rather than in the church. The wedding would be on Saturday and the couple would be back at work on Monday.

Mr Pagan would prefer to marry people in church but in his opinion the most important consideration is that they should be genuinely seeking a Christian marriage. Ian and Wendy were both parishioners, so he knew them, felt he had a duty to them and, having talked to them about their commitment, he decided there was no real reason why he should not go along with Neil's wishes. He also agreed to keep the venue secret from Wendy.

The marriage of Neil and Wendy McBride was an historic occasion, being the first legal wedding to be held in the Old Blacksmith's Shop since 1940. It was even more unique than that for it was the first Christian marriage to be held there – ever.

'I enjoyed performing the wedding in such novel surroundings, but I don't propose to make a habit of this kind of ceremony,' said the Rev Pagan.

Since then he has taken more weddings in the Old Blacksmith's Shop, each time giving considerable thought to the couple who have asked for this favour. He meets them two or three times, at least, and gets to know them and questions their commitment to assure himself as far as possible they are not taking marriage lightly because of the unusual venue. He is, however, all too aware that with every marriage there is an element of risk wherever it is celebrated.

The more recent weddings have taken place very early in the morning, before 8.30 am but even so the first coachload of tourists have arrived by the time the service is over and the party is leaving the Smithy. In his previous ten years in Scotland, the Rev Pagan has only twice been asked to conduct a wedding other than in the church, and on those occasions the service has been in hotels where the reception was to be held.

Within a year of that first wedding, another couple chose to be married over the anvil in a real religious ceremony. William McCarton and Rhona Plunkett from Annan also decided on the famous Old Blacksmith's Shop for their wedding in October 1986, because they wanted something different, something romantic.

'The marriage service is sacred in itself, not because of the place in which it is performed,' explained the Rev Bill Ferguson of Annan Old Parish Church. 'Therefore I had no difficulty in taking part in this ceremony in the Blacksmith's Shop.'

The bride wore a white wedding gown and veil and glowed with happiness as she entered the Smithy on the arm of her father, who was dressed in his kilt. She was attended by two bridesmaids and a flower girl. About forty guests squeezed into the dusty old forge, with its pictures of old 'priests' and yellowing cuttings of runaway weddings. The ceremony included the singing of Psalm 23, unaccompanied, and several special prayers.

The bridegroom, a fitter and turner, said, 'People come from all over the world to see Gretna Green Smithy, and as we live near we thought it was a good idea to get married there.' They both agreed it had been a wonderful day.

Another real wedding ceremony took place in April 1988, when a young American couple were married in the Old Blacksmith's Shop by

Adam Barr, the twenty-one year old minister of the Church of Christ in Cumbernauld.

Jeff Brown and Diane Ridley, both aged twenty-eight came from Huntville, Alabama, USA, and they felt that it would be lovely to go to Scotland for their wedding. The church to which they belong has close links with the church in Cumbernauld and they had made friends with Mr Barr the previous year when he was studying in the States. They had never heard of Gretna Green but when he told them about its history of runaway couples they were fascinated.

Mr Barr had never before conducted a wedding, and hastily sent off for a licence. Jeff and Diane told only their parents and two of the church elders. They stood behind the anvil for the ceremony and although there were few guests they sang several hymns, as well as 'The Lord is My Shepherd'. Mr Barr takes the view that a marriage is between the two people and God. The place does not really matter. He added, 'If I'd known it was customary to clang the hammer on the anvil I would probably have done that too!'

'We thought it was neat to have the wedding in the old Smithy,' said Diane. 'This is something we shall remember all our lives – just wait till we tell our friends back home.'

They could stay only a few days before flying back to resume work. Jeff is a landscaper and part owner of The Boston Celtics, a professional baseball team.

Some ministers refuse to have anything to do with the Gretna scene, but undoubtedly those marriages in the Old Blacksmith's Shop have created a precedent. It seems quite likely there will be more, for many of today's young couples are as romantic as ever their forebears were. Emotion glows in their faces as they join hands over the anvil and make their vows – intensified by the idea that they are linking their loves to those of the countless thousands who have stood there before them.

Gretna Green is an extraordinary place. You can make of it what you will. All the vices and virtues that exist in the human soul have been revealed in its stories and only a microscopic amount has been recorded about those who have been drawn there to make vows, one to another. Love is the most intangible of human emotions but in Gretna the truth and reality of its existence cannot be denied. Today, as much as ever – perhaps even more than ever – Gretna spins around its weddings.

# JOCK OF HAZELDEAN

Why weep ye by the tide, ladie,
   Why weep ye by the tide?
I'll wed ye to my youngest son,
   And ye sall be his bride,
And ye sall be his bride, ladie,
   Sae comely to be seen' –
But aye she loot the tears down fa'
   For Jock of Hazeldean.

Now let this wilfu' grief be done,
   And dry that cheek so pale;
Young Frank is chief of Errington,
   And lord of Langley-dale;
His step is first in peaceful ha',
   His sword in battle keen' –
But aye she loot the tears down fa'
   For Jock of Hazeldean.

The kirk was deck'd at morning-tide,
   The tapers glimmer'd fair,
The priest and bridegroom wait the bride,
   And dame and knight are there.
They sought her baith by bower and ha';
   The ladie was not seen!
She's o'er the Border, and awa'
   Wi' Jock of Hazeldean.

*Sir Walter Scott*

# Bibliography

Henry, Warren, *Gretna Green Romances* (Cecil Palmer 1926)

'Claverhouse', *Irregular Border Marriages* (The Moray Press 1934)

Walton, F B, *Scotch Marriages, Regular and Irregular* (Wm Green & Sons 1893)

Hutchinson, Peter Orlando, *Chronicles of Gretna Green* (Richard Bentley 1844)

Stone, Lawrence, *The Family, Sex and Marriage in England 1500–1800* (Weidenfeld & Nicholson 1977)

Tute, Warren, *Cochrane – A life of Admiral the Earl of Dundonald* (Cassel 1965)

Thomas, Donald, *Cochrane – Britannia's Last Sea-King* (Deutsch 1978)

Grimble, Ian, *The Sea Wolf: Life of Admiral Cochrane* (Blond & Briggs 1978)

Dundonald, Thomas, 10th Earl of, *Autobiography of a Seaman* (2 volumes 1860)

House of Lords Sessions Papers – Dundonald Peerage Claim 1861–63

Garnett, R, *Edward Gibbon Wakefield* (1898)

Harrop, A J, *The Amazing Career of Edward Gibbon Wakefield* (1928)

Bloomfield, Paul, *Edward Gibbon Wakefield* (Longmans 1961)

*Memoire of Sydney Smith By His Daughter, with selected letters* (1855)

New, Chester W, *The Life of Henry Brougham to 1830* (Clarendon Press 1961)

Hawes, Frances, *Henry Brougham* (1957)

Surtees, W E, *A Sketch of the lives of Lords Stowell and Eldon* (1846)

Price, F G Hilton, *Handbook of London Bankers* (1890–1)

Morrison, William, *Border Sketches*

McDougall, Richard P, *The Gretna Blacksmith's Story* (Hugh Mackie 1928)

Elliot, Robert, *Memoires of Gretna Green* (1842)

Hyslop, Robert, *Echoes from the Border Hills* (1912)

Burn, J S, *History of Fleet Marriages* (1833)

Dewar, Peter de V B, *The House of Nell Gwynn 1670–1974* (Kimber 1974)

# Index